THE COMPLETE BOOK OF
FLOWERPOT ECOLOGY

Chamber of Commerce
1-573-783-2604
Fredericktown, Mo.

THE COMPLETE BOOK OF
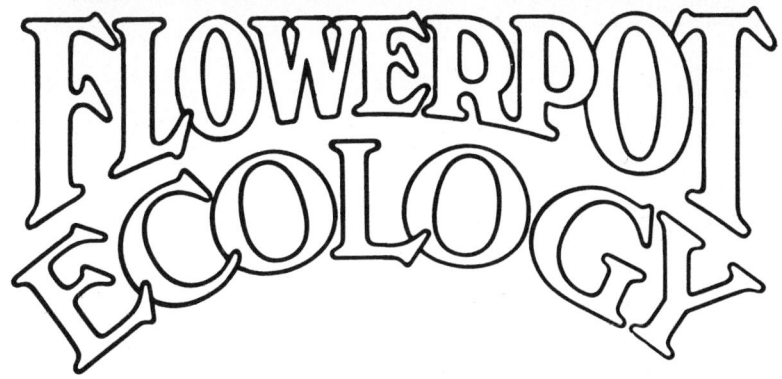

ANNA B. GESMER
AND
ELISABETH GITTER

Illustrated by Elisabeth Gitter

COWARD, McCANN & GEOGHEGAN, INC.
NEW YORK

Copyright ©1975 by Anna B. Gesmer and Elisabeth Gitter

All rights reserved. This book, or parts thereof, may not be reproduced in any form without permission in writing from the publisher. Published on the same day in Canada by Longman Canada Limited, Toronto.

SBN: 698-10614-8
Library of Congress Catalog Card Number: 74-79696

Printed in the United States of America

For Joe, Eda, and Max

PREFACE

This book is written for parents, teachers, day-care group leaders, camp counselors, and other adults who work with children. Older children will be able to do most of these projects by themselves or with minimal supervision, and city dwellers of any age may want to create windowsill gardens using some of the ideas presented here.

The projects in this book require very little space or money, and most of them can be completed quickly. They are designed to encourage children to use their ingenuity to find among the articles they would normally throw away the materials for creating new plant life. The purpose of the book is twofold: through active, varied, and interesting projects, it introduces children to nature's cycles, at the same time teaching them to look for their own ways to cycle and recycle.

The emphasis throughout is ecological: By doing these projects, the child learns about reproductive, nutritional, hydrological, and biogeochemical cycles, and about the meaning of the phrase "chain of life." He sees how plants perpetuate themselves and adapt to their environments, and discovers what they contribute to their communities as well as what they use up.

The arrangement of the projects, which deal in turn with seeds, methods of vegetative propagation, and various types of ecological communities, is biologically logical. Each section of projects is followed by explanations, in question-and-answer form, that anticipate the questions children might ask about what they are doing and observing. These explanations are designed to help the teacher or parent show the child what biological and ecological principles are illustrated by each project.

Since children like to see quick results, most of the plants recommended in this book will grow in a few days. Many of the results are dramatic: The child sees that he can grow his own fruits, vegetables, or trees from seeds that he has gathered himself, and that he can make a whole new plant from a tiny piece of an old one. Finally, and most important, in doing these projects the child will not be disappointed by unaccountable failure; the projects have all been tested and retested by the authors to ensure that they actually work.

Contents

GETTING STARTED: THE ECOLOGICAL DOUBLE TAKE
Recycling throwaways
into gardening tools   15

PART ONE: SEEDS
  I. Where Do All the Flowers Go?
Learning about the flowering cycle
through projects with seeds   25
    PROJECTS
    1. *A Seed Hunt*   29
    2. *Tumbler Gardens*   32
    3. *Anatomy of a Seed*   33
    4. *Potato Heads*   36
    5. *Egg-Carton Gardens*   37
    6. *Sponge Gardens*   39
    7. *Plastic-Bottle Strawberry Jars*   40
    8. *Citrus Groves*   43
    9. *Vine salad "Trees"*   45
    10. *Avocados*   47

  Some Questions and Answers
About Seeds   51

II. Minifarms: Growing Vegetables
    at Home   61
How It's Done   62

*Some Questions and Answers
About Minivegetable Gardening*   72

III. Miniforests: Finding out how mighty
     oaks from little acorns grow   75
How It's Done   77

*Some Questions and Answers
About Trees*   83

PART TWO: REPRODUCING PLANTS WITHOUT SEEDS

IV. New Plants from Old Stems   87
    PROJECTS
    1. A Trading Slips Club (stem tip
       cuttings)   89
    2. Stolon Fruits (runners or stolons)   95
    3. Rhizome Rearing (underground stems)   96
    4. A Potato Patch (tubers)   99
    5. An Onion Bouquet (bulbs)   100
    6. April in February (forcing bulbs)   102

*Some Questions and Answers
About Stems*   105

V. Stirring Dull Roots — 109
   PROJECTS
   1. Root Division — 110
   2. A Sweet Potato Vine — 112
   3. A Carrot and Beet Garden — 115
   4. A Carrot-Hanging Basket — 116

   Some Questions and Answers
   About Roots — 119

VI. Turning Over a New Leaf — 121
   PROJECTS
   1. Starting Leaf Cuttings in Soil — 122
   2. Two Ways to Start Leaf Cuttings
      in Water — 124
   3. Bits That Grow Big — 126
   4. Triangles — 128
   5. In the Same Vein—an Instant
      Begonia Garden — 130

   Some Questions and Answers
   About Leaf Cuttings — 132

PART THREE: PLANTS AND THEIR COMMUNITIES

VII. Ecosystems — 137
   PROJECTS
   1. Building a Terrarium Case — 139

    2. *A Desert Terrarium*   145
    3. *A Woodland Terrarium*   146
    4. *A Cultivated Garden Terrarium*   153
    5. *A Bog Terrarium*   155
    6. *Dish Gardens*   158

Some Questions and Answers About Terraria and Plant Communities   163

APPENDICES

    A. Common Poisonous House Plants   167
    B. Where to Send for Plants and Supplies   169

INDEX   171

THE COMPLETE BOOK OF

FLOWERPOT ECOLOGY

GETTING STARTED: THE ECOLOGICAL DOUBLE TAKE

A little ingenuity and imagination can produce almost all the materials needed for the projects in this book. All you need to do is look over your trash with an inventive eye toward what can be salvaged and reused. We call this doing an ecological double take.

Begin by looking with your child or children for possible plant containers. Paper and styrofoam cups, plastic margarine tubs, cans of all sizes, and milk cartons can all become flowerpots. Aluminum frozen-food tins and plastic egg cartons make good flats for getting seeds started. Plastic bleach, detergent, ammonia, and shampoo bottles are not biodegradable but can easily be transformed with a

A hanging basket made from a berry box and planted with Swedish ivy.

Panty-hose containers strung together to make a window planter.

scissors into attractive planters. Save leaky pails, old dishpans, and dented trash cans for larger plants.

Pretty hanging baskets can be made from straw or plastic berry boxes. Line the basket with a sheet of plastic, then simply tie strings of equal length to the four sides of the basket, and tie the strings together at the top. A coconut cut in half and hollowed out, an Italian wine basket, a small colander, or a string of cans or egg-shaped panty-hose containers can all be hung as window planters.

The key to transforming empty containers into planters is providing drainage. Without some way for it to drain off, excess water accumulates at the bottom of the pot, and the soil becomes so soggy that air cannot penetrate. This diminishes the supply of oxygen to the roots and the plant "smothers" to death. The best way to provide drainage is to punch three holes in the bottom of your container. Cover the holes with bottle caps or pieces of broken crockery, hollow side down, to keep the soil from falling out. Solid plastic containers like those used for ice cream hold up better if you punch the holes along the sides, about a quarter-inch from the bottom, rather than on the bottom itself. Clear plastic glasses are good for small plants and cuttings. It is not hard to provide these with drainage. Briefly heat a corn-on-the-cob holder or a nail with a match and punch holes in the bottom of the glass. Some people use heated ice picks for this, but that idea makes us nervous.

Now try to assemble a supply of recycled gardening tools to use in the projects. This step might be presented to children as a kind of treasure hunt. Here are some suggestions:

Popsicle sticks are handy stakes for seedlings.

Save the string from bakery boxes or laundry packages to tie up vines.

The clear plastic bags that lettuce and bread come wrapped in are very useful. Slip flats of seeds inside the bags to create a moist greenhouse environment. If

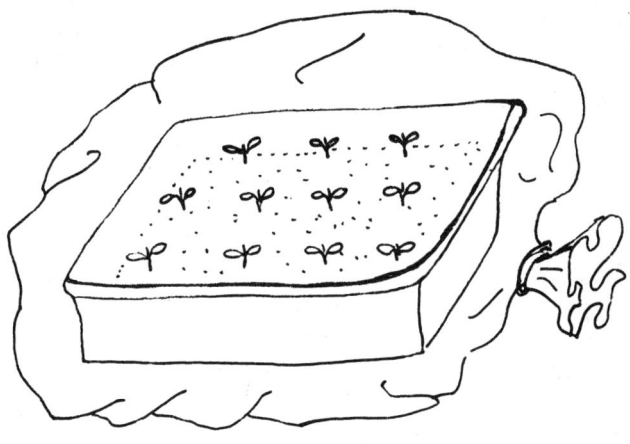

A flat of seeds sprouting inside a plastic-bag minigreenhouse.

you have to go away and leave plants, keep them in plastic bags and they will survive up to three weeks. Cleaners' bags are good for large plants. (But be sure to keep plants in plastic out of direct sunlight, or they will cook!)

A layer of bottle caps at the bottom of pots provides good drainage. If they rust, all the better; they will enrich the soil with iron.

Used aluminum foil torn in pieces and rolled into pebble-sized balls makes useful synthetic gravel.

Save glass jars for tumbler gardens and for starting cuttings in water.

Wash out spray bottles—the kind Windex and some detergents come in—and refill them with water. Use these sprays to mist moisture-loving plants and to wash leaves.

To make your own plant fertilizer, save eggshells. Crush them, cover them with water, and store the mixture in a covered container. After a week you will have an excellent (though smelly) mild fertilizer.

For some of the projects in this book you may wish to buy seeds or small plants, but you can always make do with the parts of food you normally throw away: the tops of radishes, carrots, beets, and turnips; the eyes of potatoes; the seeds of cucumbers, apples, grapes, melons, avocados, squash, oranges, and other fruits.

Once you have mastered the ecological double take, all you will need to buy is soil. Of course you could dig some up from a yard or park, but it might contain fungus or insect pests, and would not be porous enough for potted plants. Unlike outdoor plants, plants confined to pots do not have their soil turned regularly by worms and burrowing insects; their roots will not get enough oxygen unless the plants are potted in a lighter mixture that will not pack and harden. For convenience we recommend the packaged synthetic soils that are sterile mixtures of vermiculite, peat moss, perlite, and fertilizers. Commercial potting soil, which is mostly humus, is also sterile, but tends to pack or cake. It needs to be mixed with peat moss and coarse sand, vermiculite, or perlite.

If you teach your children to be resourceful double takers, they can garden for less than a dollar while learning to recycle. It will be satisfying and exciting for them to see that they can have attractive, fruitful plants without having to ask for money to buy them. And it is important for them to learn that not everything that is thrown away is trash.

PART ONE
SEEDS

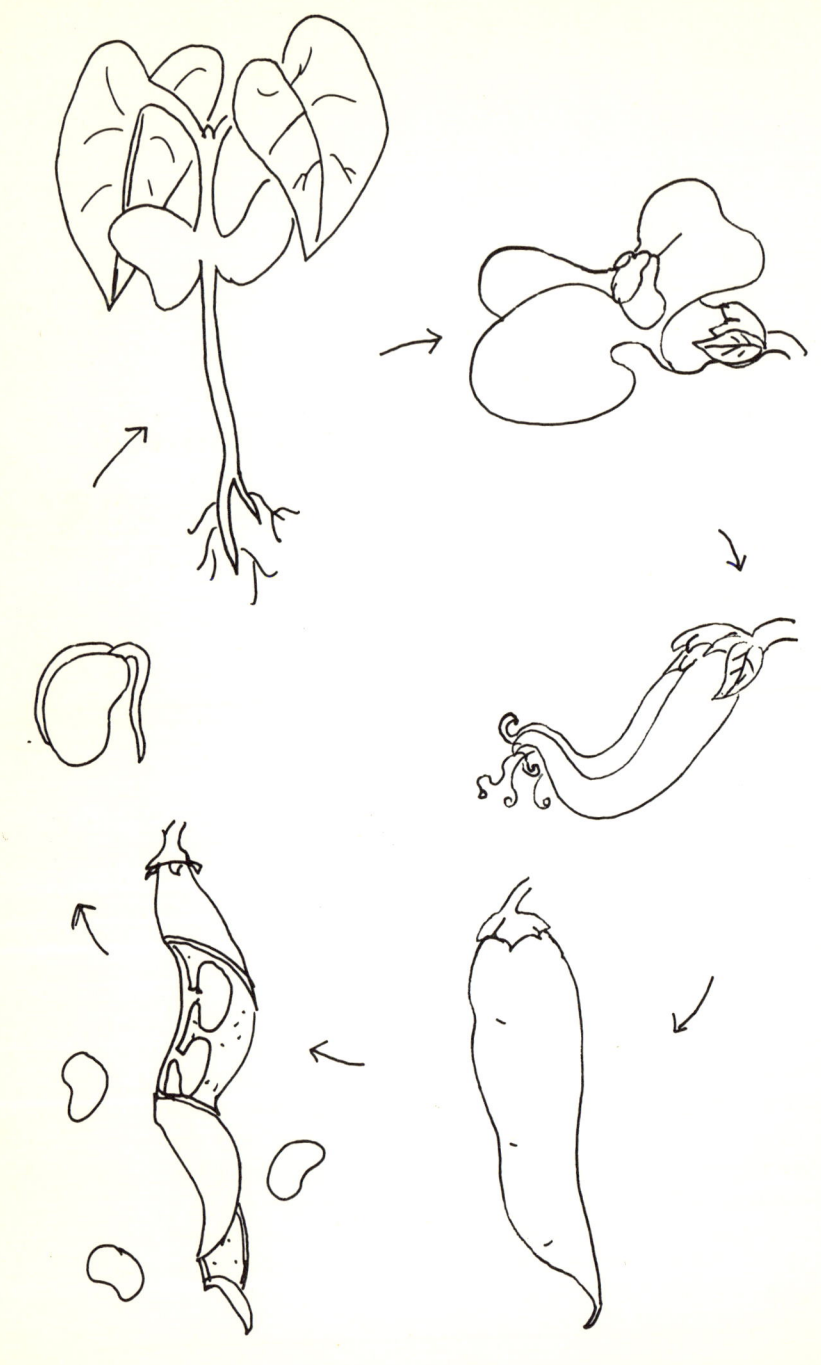

Chapter I

Where Do All the Flowers Go?

Unlike old soldiers, old flowers don't just fade away—they go to seed. The seeds developed from the flower grow into new plants, the new plants produce flowers, the flowers make seeds, and the cycle begins again.

The life cycle of the bean. The seed (shown on the left) sprouts into a plant with roots and shoots, and the plant flowers. After pollination, when the ovules have been fertilized, the external parts of the flower wither and the ovary begins to enlarge as the ovules develop. The bean pod (lower right) is the enlarged ovary, the beans inside it are the ovules. If left on the plant, the pod will dry up and expel its seeds, which will sprout and begin the cycle again.

This is only one of the many cycles that maintain life on our planet. Through this cycle each species of plant preserves itself. Even though dandelions may be picked or mown or eaten by animals, enough of them go to seed to ensure that as long as there are even a few patches of green left in the world, there will be golden dandelions poking up in the spring.

Before we explore the flowering cycle further, it might be a good idea to define the terms we will be using. A *seed,* to begin at the beginning, is the part of a flowering plant that contains the embryo of a new plant; it also has stored food to nourish the developing embryo and a coating to protect it. In scientific terms it is a fertilized ovule.

The *flower* is the seed-producing structure of a plant. Flowers vary tremendously in the way they look and in the way they function. Some flowers have exotic fragrances and brilliantly colored petals; others, such as the flowers of many trees and grasses, are inconspicuous. Many plants have flowers with both male and female parts, but some species have separate male flowers, which produce pollen, and female flowers, which contain ovules. In either case the process of fertilization is the same: A sperm cell from a grain of pollen must fuse with an ovule; the result is a seed.

A *fruit* is a seed vessel. In botanical language it is the ripened ovary of a flower and contains the fertilized ovule, or seed. There are many kinds of fruits: fleshy fruits, such as the blueberry, tomato, cucumber, apple, and pear; stone fruits, such as the cherry, plum, and peach; and dry fruits, such as the acorn, bean, walnut, and, most important for feeding the world, grain.

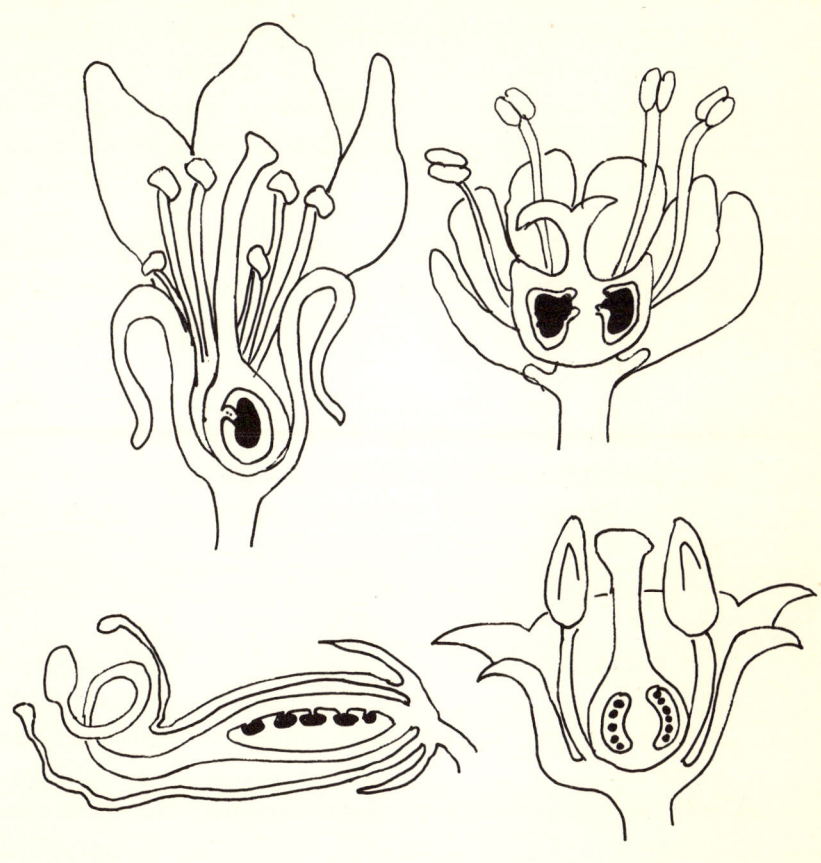

Cross sections of typical flowers, showing the ovules in their ovaries. The cherry flower (upper left) has one ovule; the maple (upper right) has two; the bean (lower left) and potato (lower right) have many ovules.

Some people are confused about the distinction between fruits and vegetables. *Vegetable* is actually a very broad term: any part of a plant or the plant itself is vegetable—as opposed to animal or inorganic. To make the distinction clear to children you might pose this riddle: "Why is it that all fruits are vegetables, but not all vegetables are fruits?"

Although most of the plants we readily think of produce flowers, we should remember that the great majority of the world's plants reproduce by other means. Molds, yeast, fungi, algae, lichens, seaweed, mosses, horsetails, and ferns are all flowerless and seedless. They multiply in a variety of complex ways: through spores, reproductive swellings, and vegetative propagation.

COMPLETE BOOK OF FLOWERPOT ECOLOGY

PROJECTS

1. A Seed Hunt

Seeds come in all sizes. Some are as fine as dust; others, coconuts, for example, are pretty hefty. One species of coconut from the Seychelles Islands produces seeds that weigh up to fifty pounds! It is exciting to children to discover this almost infinite variety for themselves. They will be amazed at how much of the food they eat is really seeds: A family of five eats an average of forty pounds of seeds in one week!

Indoors: Take a tour of your kitchen or supermarket, looking for the many seeds we eat: rice, corn, barley, chick-peas, lima beans, peas, and nuts. Have each child make a list, including foods made from such seeds as flour, coffee, and chocolate. Cut open apples, pears, peaches, cherries, berries, squash, and tomatoes and examine and compare the various sizes and shapes of seeds they bear. Wash the seeds, let them dry out, and store them for future planting.

Out-of-doors: Have each child collect as many kinds of seeds as he can find: acorns, chestnuts, pine nuts (in their cones), maple seeds (with their winglike "propellers"), dandelion and milkweed fluffy "parachutes," beechnuts, and thistles. Each kind of seed has its own dispersal equipment: Maples are propelled by the wind on their wings, dandelions on their parachutes, burrs stick to passersby (animal and human), who carry them to other neighborhoods; nuts and acorns are carried off and buried—or planted—by squirrels. Try to identify the dispersal apparatus of each seed found.

Some of the seed-bearing fruits to look for on a kitchen seed hunt.

Some of the seeds and seed-bearing fruits to look for on an outdoor seed hunt. Above, from left to right, are a dandelion seed, with its "parachute," maple seeds with their "propellers," and the seeds of the vetch in their pods. Below, left to right, are a blackberry, a beggar's tick, and a cocklebur.

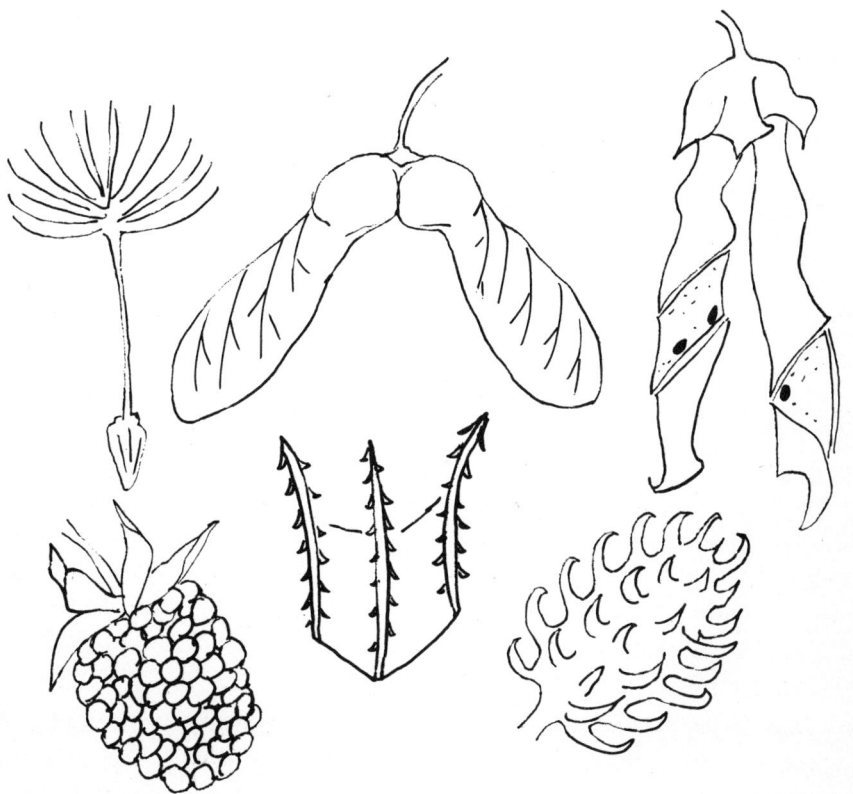

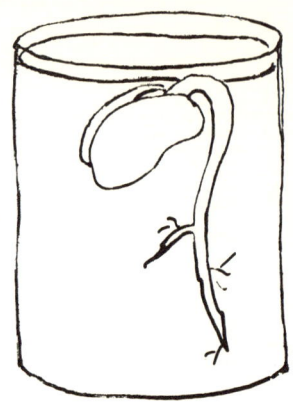

A bean seed sprouting in a tumbler garden.

2. Tumbler Gardens

This easy project produces quick results and is suitable for young children. It is an excellent teaching tool because it shows so clearly the process of germination, or sprouting.

Equipment:
1. A clear glass tumbler (a jelly glass works well).
2. Blotting paper or paper towel.
3. Cotton batting.
4. Beans or lentils.
5. Unpopped popcorn (or dried corn kernels).

COMPLETE BOOK OF FLOWERPOT ECOLOGY

Method:
1. Soak the seeds in water overnight.
2. Line the glass with the blotting paper or paper towel, wetting it so that it sticks to the sides of the glass.
3. Stuff some cotton batting in the bottom of the glass and moisten it. This will keep the paper moist.
4. Place the seeds between the glass and the blotting paper, about a third of the distance from the top. Three bean seeds and three corn seeds make an interesting beginning.
5. Put the glass in a spot away from direct sunlight. Keep the cotton in the bottom moist enough so the blotting paper never dries out, but do not drench it.
6. As soon as the seeds begin to germinate or sprout, move the tumbler to a sunny window.

Results: In a few days the roots will start to grow down and the shoot will grow up. The little plants will not thrive longer than two weeks unless they are planted in pots.

3. Anatomy of a Seed

This project, for children over eight, should be done in conjunction with Project 2, which it explains and enriches.

Equipment:
1. Several beans and corn kernels.
2. A magnifying glass.
3. A small dish of water.

34 COMPLETE BOOK OF FLOWERPOT ECOLOGY

Method:
1. Soak the beans and corn kernels in water overnight, and then examine them with the magnifying glass. Point out the place where the bean was attached to the pod. Look for the pinhole above this, where the young root is going to push through.
2. Now peel the seed coats. Point out that the bean is made of two parts, or cotyledons (cot-ee-*lee*-dons). A plant with two cotyledons—the bean, for example—is called a dicotyledon. The cotyledons give the plant the energy it needs to start growing, and will nourish it until it has produced enough leaves and roots to sustain itself.

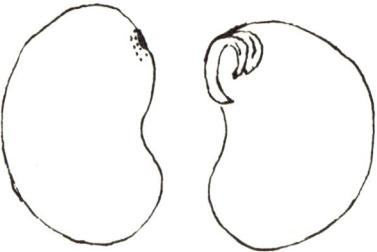

Separated cotyledons of the bean. Attached to the cotyledon on the right are the small root, stem, and leaves. The leaves hide the tiny bud.

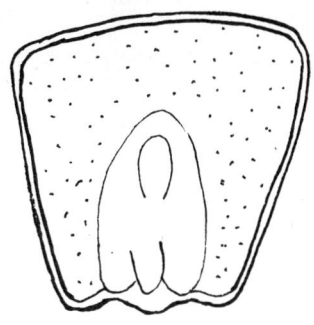

Cross section of a kernel of corn, a monocotyledon, revealing the embryo.

3. Separate the two cotyledons to expose the tiny plant embryo safely tucked between them. The little folded leaves will grow into the green shoot and the pointed part will become the root.
4. Now look at the corn. It does not split in two as the bean does because it has only one cotyledon. Plants like corn are called monocotyledons. The light section of the corn kernel is the cotyledon. The dark yellow part of the kernel nourishes the corn as it grows. Point out the little raised ridge on the cotyledon. The top of the ridge will grow into the shoot and the bottom will grow into the root.

All seeds are either monocotyledons or dicotyledons, and the characteristics you have observed in the corn and bean appear in all seeds. The advantage of using corn and bean seeds is that they are large, easy to handle and see, and readily available.

4. Potato Heads

This project is fun for young children, and produces results in just a few days.

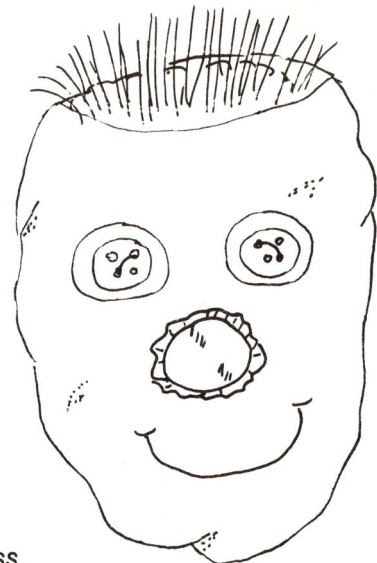

A potato head planted with grass.

Equipment:
1. A large potato.
2. Quick-growing seeds—lettuce, mustard, and cress (which can be clipped as they grow and used in salads), or grass. For a redhead, use *Ruby* variety lettuce.
3. For eyes, two buttons secured with hairpins.
4. For a nose, a cork or carrot end secured with a toothpick, or a bottle top pressed into the potato.
5. Red paint or crayon to draw a mouth.
6. Several bottle tops or a needle holder to make a stand for the potato.
7. A wad of cotton or a sponge.

Method:
1. Slice a piece from one end of the potato and hollow out some of the center.
2. Fill the hollow with a large wad of well-moistened cotton or sponge.
3. Design the potato's "face."
4. Generously sprinkle the cotton or sponge with seeds.
5. Press the bottom of the potato into the needle holder or bottle tops so that the "head" stays up. If you prefer, slice off the end of the potato to make a flat base.
6. Watch carefully to make sure the wadding doesn't dry out. Results: The potato will grow a head of "hair" in a few days. When its "hair" grows too long, trim it and use the clippings in salads. Depending on the temperature of the room it is kept in, your potato head should last from two weeks to well over a month without spoiling. For a long-lasting project, keep a cool head!

5. *Egg Carton Gardens*

This project produces attractive planters, which children can present as gifts or use to decorate their own homes.

Equipment:
1. One egg carton.
2. Twelve eggshells. You can save the shells as you use the eggs; they will keep indefinitely. Or make an omelet the day you do this project.
3. Seeds of beans, peas, lentils, nasturtiums, dwarf-sized marigolds, or zinnias.
4. Soil.
5. Crayons.

An egg carton garden planted with peas.

Method:
1. Unless they are tiny, soak the seeds in water overnight.
2. Cut the top off the carton.
3. Color the outside of the carton with crayon for decoration.
4. Crack the eggs, leaving the broad end larger, and pour out the contents. You need not wash the shells.
5. Fill the larger half of each shell three-quarters full of soil and put it back in its own compartment in the carton.
6. Poke a hole with your finger in the soil of each egg, drop in a seed, and cover it lightly with more soil.
7. Water the seeds lightly with a bulb spray or syringe. Do not let them dry out.

Results: In a few days the little plants will appear. If all twelve do not show up, drop in another seed. When the shoots come up, put the carton in good light, and when the true leaves appear, move it to a sunny spot. Turn the carton every day so the plants will grow evenly. When the plants begin to look crowded, they may be transplanted, shell and all, to small pots. The shell will serve as fertilizer.

6. *Sponge Gardens*

These attractive gardens make excellent centerpieces and grow quickly.

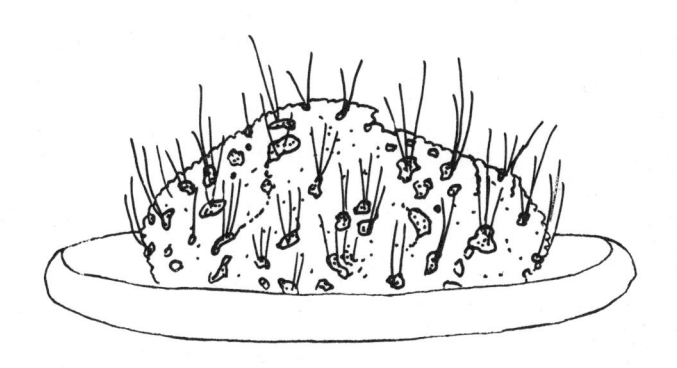

Grass growing in a sponge garden.

Equipment:
   1. A sponge, preferably natural, which is prettier, although the synthetic type works just as well. Natural sponges can be purchased in art-supply stores, in bath-accessory shops, and in house painters' supply stores.
   2. A shallow dish, saucer, or ashtray.

3. A clear plastic or glass bowl large enough to fit over the shallow dish, or a plastic bag.
4. Lettuce, cress, grass, or rye seed, mixed birdseed, or parakeet seed. (If you use wild bird seed, make sure that the label does not say that it has been heated to kill the plant embryo, a practice that began with the discovery that the birdseed sometimes contains the seeds of *Cannabis,* or marijuana.)

Method:
1. Soak the sponge and set it in the shallow dish, which should be half full of water.
2. Sprinkle the seed generously over the sponge. Some seeds will fall into the holes; press in the others with a popsicle stick.
3. Cover the dish and sponge with the clear bowl, or slip them into a plastic bag so that the seeds will not dry out.
4. Check periodically to make sure there is water in the dish.
5. When the seeds start to sprout, remove the cover or bag and put the sponge garden in a sunny window.

Results: Within a week the seeded sponge grows into an attractive miniature garden. The cress and mustard plants can be clipped and added to salads and sandwiches.

7. *Plastic-Bottle Strawberry Jars*

The ancestors of the terra-cotta strawberry jars so popular today were barrels with openings in the sides, which were used in English gardens to grow strawberries. Now, regardless of what is grown in it, we call any container with openings in the sides a "strawberry jar"—even a plastic bottle!

How to make a plastic bottle strawberry jar: Prepare the bottle by cutting off the top and cutting out crescents from the sides, as shown on the left. Dwarf geraniums grow out of the openings in the completed strawberry jar on the right.

This project requires the use of a scissors or knife, so young children will need some help.

Equipment:
1. An empty half-gallon or gallon plastic bottle. Bleach bottles with tear-off labels are prettiest, but detergent, shampoo, or spring-water bottles work as well. Try to find a bottle without a handle.
2. Knife or scissors.
3. Crayon or pencil.
4. Pebbles or perlite.
5. Charcoal.
6. Packaged potting soil.
7. Seeds of kitchen herbs (sage, mint, thyme, parsley, or savory look prettiest and are useful); dwarf tomatoes or cucumbers; or low growing flowers (dwarf impatiens, lobelia, sweet alyssum, nasturtiums, and vinca work well).

Method:
1. Wash out the bottle carefully.
2. At different heights, with a pencil or crayon, draw crescent shapes on the bottle. The crescents should be two inches across.
3. Cut out the shapes with a knife or sharp scissors.
4. Pour in a half-inch layer of pebbles or perlite for drainage at the bottom of the bottle, and a few small pieces of charcoal to keep the soil sweet.
6. Fill the container with potting soil.
7. Press the seeds into the soil through the cut-out openings.
8. Water from the top.

Results: The seeds will sprout through the openings, transforming the bottle into a pretty strawberry jar.

8. Citrus Groves

It is not unusual for children to think of seeds as little commercial items that come in boxes and envelopes, and not as vital links in the chain of life. One of the best ways to correct this impression and to illustrate the continuities in nature is to have children grow new plants from the seeds of fruit they have eaten.

Citrus-fruit seeds give quick results usually within two weeks. All citrus seeds, but tangerine and grapefruit seeds in particular, germinate easily. After four or five years the plants, which have striking dark green foliage, will blossom and even bear fruit. Unfortunately the new fruit is usually not very tasty, but it does dramatize the flowering cycle.

Equipment:
1. Seeds of grapefruit, lemons, limes, fresh kumquats, tangerines, or oranges.
2. Containers: styrofoam coffee cups, paper cups, juice or soup cans, emptied and washed out for small groves; for larger groves use frozen-cake tins or milk cartons with one side cut away.
3. Sandy soil.

Method:
1. Save up about twenty of the plumpest seeds. Wash them, put them in a plastic bag, and store them in a cool place until ready for use. Unless they have begun to sprout they can be stored indefinitely.
2. Soak the seeds in water at room temperature for twelve to twenty-four hours.
3. Fill the containers with soil up to about one and a half inches from the rim.

An orange tree grown from seed.

4. Place the seeds pointed end up in the containers, about one inch apart.
5. Cover the seeds with one-quarter inch of soil or plain sand.
6. Moisten thoroughly.
7. Cover the top of the container with plastic or waxed paper and secure it with a rubber band.
8. Place the container in a warm, dark place until the seeds sprout; then bring it to light and remove the cover.

Results: The seedlings will grow quickly. When they get to be about four inches tall, dig them up with a fork, keeping the soil ball around the roots intact, and transplant them. The new containers should, of course, be provided with drainage holes.

9. *Vine Salad "Trees"*

The seeds of watermelons, grapes, cucumbers, squash, peas, beans, and melons of all kinds germinate easily and produce quick-growing vines. This project is a good complement to the citrus-grove project. In each the child sees the connection between fruit, seed, and plant, but by doing the two projects together or in sequence, he learns something of the variety of plant forms.

You can grow a fruit-salad "tree," using melon or grape seeds, or a green-salad "tree," using cucumber, pea, bean, or squash seeds. Either kind of salad "tree" will grow luxuriant foliage, but if you want your plants to flower and bear fruit indoors, peas and beans are your safest bet. Grapes will germinate but are often attacked by fungi in the soil: we do not recommend them as highly as the other vines.

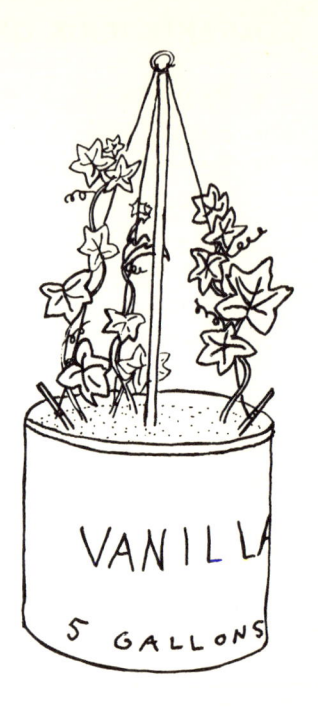

A cucumber salad "tree."

To start vines, wash off the seeds you and the children have collected with tepid water and allow them to dry out for a day or two. Then follow the potting and planting procedure outlined for Citrus Groves in Project 8.

Once the second set of leaves appears, usually within a week of sprouting, the plants are ready to be trained to grow into attractive "salad trees."

Equipment:
1. A five-gallon pickle tin from the delicatessen, a preserves container from a bakery, or an ice-cream bucket from an ice-cream parlor.
2. A sturdy pole, four to five feet high. A mop handle, broomstick, or curtain rod will work well.
3. An eye-hook.

4. Heavy twine.
5. Potting soil.
6. Several young cucumber, watermelon, squash, or other vines. To avoid confusion, use only one kind of seedling in each container.
7. As many lollipop or ice-cream-bar sticks as you have plants.
8. Crayons or paint.

Method:
1. Provide your container with drainage either by punching holes in the bottom or by spreading a layer of gravel.
2. Stand the pole in the center of the container and pour soil around it up to an inch or so from the rim. The soil should brace the pole firmly.
3. Dig holes in the soil at equal distances around the pole and set in the young plants. Press the soil back firmly around the plants.
4. Insert the eye-hook into the top of the pole.
5. String lengths of the twine from this hook down to each plant. Use the lollipop sticks as stakes to anchor the twine beside each plant.
6. Water the plants thoroughly and continue to water them as needed. Keep the container in a sunny spot.
7. Decorate the container with crayons or paint.

Results: The vines will quickly clamber up the twine and around the pole, covering it with foliage and creating the effect of a tree. Eventually blossoms will appear; you may even have fruit.

10. Avocados

It seems a shame to waste the enormous seed of the avocado, when it can produce an interesting, fast-growing plant. The avocados found in supermarkets come either from Florida or California. Both types will grow, but Florida avocado seeds seem to germinate more quickly. Perhaps they are allowed to mature on the tree longer.

Equipment for Rooting:
  1. One avocado seed.
  2. Three toothpicks or nails.
  3. Glass of water.

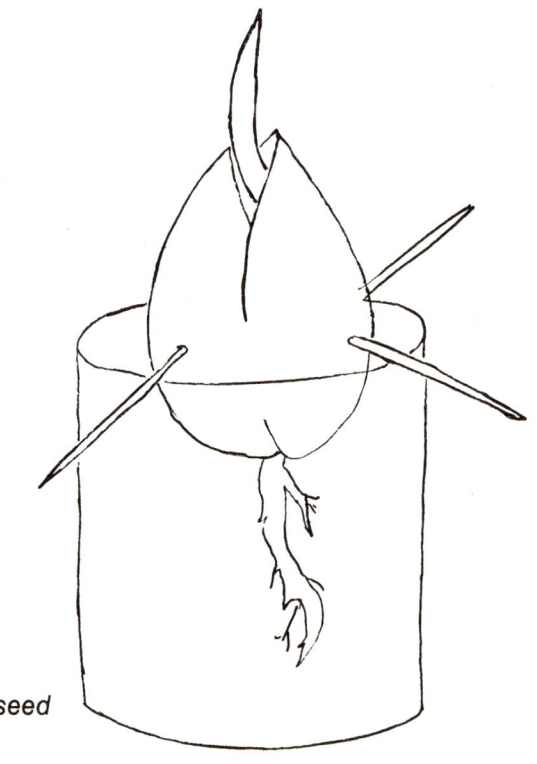

Starting an avocado seed in water.

COMPLETE BOOK OF FLOWERPOT ECOLOGY

Method for Rooting:
1. Wash the seed to remove bits of fruit that may cling to it.
2. Notice that one side of the seed is somewhat flattened. This is the bottom.
3. Insert three toothpicks or nails equidistant around the bottom half of the seed to support it in the glass.
4. Suspend the seed in the glass of water, bottom side down, so that the seed just touches the water. Maintain the water at this level.
5. Keep the seed away from draft and out of direct sunlight. Add only tepid water. The root should start growing at some time between three weeks and three months.
6. After the root appears, move the glass to full sunlight and watch for the green shoot.
7. When the root is about five inches long, it is time to pot the avocado.

Potting Equipment:
1. A large flower pot, five or six inches in diameter.
2. Drainage material.
3. Potting soil mixture.

Potting Method:
1. Put about a one-inch layer of drainage material in the bottom of the pot. Cover it with a thin layer of potting soil
2. Hold the seedling in position in the pot with one hand, so that the top of the seed will be exposed above the soil, and gradually add soil, a small amount at a time, with the other hand. The roots are brittle, so treat them gently. Jiggle the pot around and tamp it on the table to settle the soil around the roots. When all but the top of the seed is covered

An avocado seedling potted in a detergent bottle.

  with soil, water the pot thoroughly. If the soil settles down after watering, add more soil.
3. Keep the soil evenly moist at all times, and keep the plant in a sunny spot.
4. When the shoot is about ten inches tall, pinch out the growing point to make the plant bushy.
5. When the plant is about four weeks old, start fertilizing it every two weeks with a high-nitrogen fertilizer. Be sure to follow the manufacturer's directions.

Result: The avocado grows into a beautiful plant that will live for many years and grow very tall. It is rare for avocados to flower indoors; enjoy them simply for their lovely foliage.

SOME QUESTIONS AND ANSWERS ABOUT SEEDS

What makes a seed start growing?

To answer this you have to understand that a seed is really a young plant that has stopped growing. As the seed dries on the plant, its life activities slow down and almost stop. Under proper conditions seeds can remain preserved for a long time: there are stories that lotus seeds have germinated after 1,200 years!

Water brings the seed to life again. As the seed absorbs water, the life processes of the plant are activated and germination begins. Temperature also affects germination. Each kind of seed has its own temperature and moisture requirements.

Do all seeds germinate at the same speed?

No. Some seeds, like citrus fruits and peas, can germinate as soon as they form. Sometimes you can actually see sprouting seeds in pea pods and in oranges picked very ripe. Other seeds have built-in mechanisms that prevent germination before conditions are right for the plant's growth.

Is there any way to make slow seeds germinate faster?

Since seeds need to absorb a certain amount of water before they can germinate, seeds with tough coats—such as the bean or orange—can be given a quick start by soaking overnight. Grape and date pits may be soaked for a week.

Commercial growers hasten germination by mechanically scarring the surfaces of tough-coated seeds or by soaking them in sulfuric acid. You can approximate this process at home by chipping or scratching the seed coat with a nail, but be careful not to penetrate the coat or injure the plant embryo.

Why don't some seeds germinate, even when conditions are right?

Some seeds will not germinate because the embryo has been injured, either by insects, fungi, or bacteria, or by mechanical means. The rule is, treat seeds "like eggs, not stones"; otherwise, they may be injured.

Other seeds do not germinate because they seem to have a delayed-action mechanism, a built-in time clock that keeps them dormant until a second or third season rolls around. This mechanism protects the species against extinction, because if all the seedlings are killed off one year by a natural catastrophe (flood or drought), there will still be some seeds ready to germinate the following year.

Why don't roots grow up and shoots grow down when seeds are planted upside down?

COMPLETE BOOK OF FLOWERPOT ECOLOGY 53

Plants are able to respond to the pull of gravity; they exhibit what is called geotropism. Roots show positive geotropism—they grow toward the center of the earth. Stems have a negative response to gravity—they grow away from its pull. No matter how a plant is turned, these responses always occur.

An example of geotropism. Although the bulb on the right has been planted upside down, its roots have begun to grow down toward the center of the earth while the shoot, which has a negative response to gravity, is turning upward. Eventually the shoot will break ground and blossom, but not as quickly as the correctly planted bulb on the left, which does not need to change direction under ground.

Why do some seeds get moldy?

Molds, like seeds, grow best in warmth, moisture, and darkness. Most commercial seeds are treated to prevent mold, but the seeds you clean yourself may be susceptible. Take care that they do not become too wet or too warm, since fungi thrive under those conditions. If you are growing seeds you have taken from fruits or vegetables, wash them very carefully, for molds and bacteria will develop in any remaining flesh.

How deep should seeds be planted?
Seeds should be planted at a depth equal to their size. Tiny seeds are just sprinkled on the surface of the soil and pressed down. A light sprinkling of moist sand will keep them from drying out.

At what temperature should planted seeds be kept?
Generally speaking seeds germinate faster if they are kept warm. But there are exceptions. Lettuce, which is a cool-weather crop, germinates best between 65° and 75° Fahrenheit. Tropical plants like coffee seeds (which are unroasted coffee beans) will germinate only between eighty and eighty-five degrees; it is best to keep them where they can get bottom heat—on a covered radiator, for instance.

Is there any way to avoid buying soil?
Only if you are willing to go through the bother of sterilizing your own backyard or park soil. Enterprising souls can do this by taking an old roasting pan and measuring in one gallon of soil to one cup of water. Bake this mixture in a 180° F. oven for forty-five minutes. While the soil is cooling, aerate it

Preparing soil for sterilization.

by turning it out on several layers of clean newspaper. The soil should cool for twenty-four hours before you use it. This process will kill most harmful bacteria and fungi.

Why add charcoal to the pot?

Charcoal absorbs impurities from the soil solution. It is used with drainage material in the bottom of pots, where water may accumulate. It prevents molds and the unpleasant effects of decay. When a tiny piece of charcoal is placed in a vase of flowers, it keeps the water sweet-smelling.

Why does covering flats of planted seeds with plastic or glass promote growth?

If seeds dry out after they have been planted, the activated embryo is killed. Seeds that are not buried deeply are particularly likely to dry out and should always be covered.

Why should the cover be removed once the seeds sprout?

Seedlings need some circulation of air. Moreover, it gets very hot under plastic, and the plants might cook in the sunlight.

What is a true leaf?

The first leaves to appear aboveground are usually the cotyledons that nourish the growing embryo. The tiny folded leaves between the cotyledons develop later and become the first true leaves. They are easily identified by their veins. By the time these first true leaves develop, the food in the cotyledons has been used up, and they will shrivel and drop off.

Why does pinching off the growing point or terminal bud make a plant bushy?

Plant growth is controlled by hormones called auxins. Auxins stimulate growth in the terminal bud while inhibiting development of the side buds, which are present at every leaf node. Thus, the terminal bud exerts what is called apical dominance: It grows; the side buds do not. When you pinch off the terminal bud, you remove apical dominance. The side buds can then develop so that the plant will be

The bean seedling on the right still has its true leaves folded between the cotyledons. The true leaves have opened on the seedling on the left, and the cotyledons will soon begin to wither.

sturdy and well rounded, rather than tall and spindly.

Which of the seeds we find on a kitchen seed hunt will grow? Which will not?
Any untreated, mature seed will germinate. Seeds that have been roasted will not grow because excessive heat kills the plant embryo. Some plants have been hybridized to bear seeds that do not mature; these seeds will not sprout either.

Seeds that will not germinate because they have been treated include pasteurized dates and figs, polished rice, roasted coffee beans, rolled oats, barley, and groats.

The most common examples of plants that have been hybridized to bear sterile seeds are strawberries and bananas. The white seeds of watermelons are naturally immature and so will not grow.

You should have success, however, with the majority of edible seeds and seeds contained in edible fruit. Try the seeds of pomegranates, avocados, plantains (available in Spanish-American groceries), plums, cherries, persimmons, apricots, lentils, tomatoes, and cucumbers. Nuts (carefully removed from their shells), chick-peas, brown rice, unroasted coffee beans, and sunflower, poppy, carraway, and dill seeds will all sprout. Seeds from health-food stores, including barley and soy beans, are untreated and will germinate.

The rule of thumb for growing seeds is to try to duplicate the conditions under which the plants live in nature. If a plant is tropical, keep the seed warm; if it is northern, keep the seed cool. Have fun experimenting by trying to start seeds under a variety of temperature conditions. Put the seeds between layers of wet paper towels in jars and start one group in the refrigerator, a second group on a windowsill, and a third group on a radiator. Then see which group sprouts first. Since the factors affecting germination are complex, you will have some interesting results.

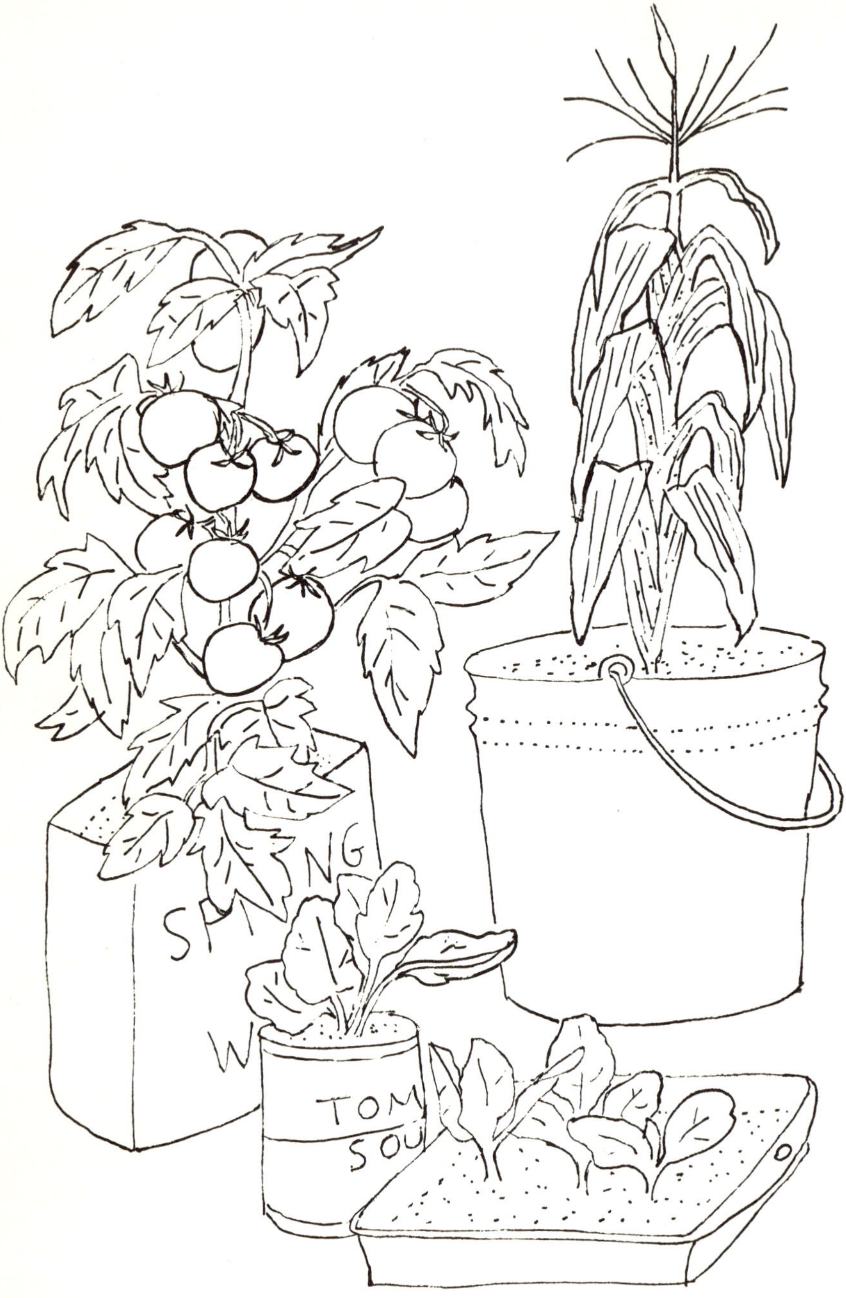
TOM
SOU

Chapter II

Minifarms: Growing Vegetables at Home

In a world where fruits and vegetables come peeled, washed, and wrapped in plastic, our dependence on plants seems remote indeed. It is hard to think of ourselves as links in a food chain when our only direct connections to food are supermarket chains. Perhaps for this reason it gives all of us—and children especially—a sense of accomplishment and pride to grow our own food.

Fortunately nowadays no one needs an acre to grow a vegetable garden. There are enough varieties of miniature vegetables available for children to grow crops on a terrace, porch, or patio. Even if they have only a windowsill or doorstep, they have enough room for a beautiful and practical minifarm.

Here's how it's done:

Find a container

Just about anything will do as a vegetable planter, as long as it fits the space you have. For a windowsill, use small containers: plastic coffee cups or cans, yogurt, cottage cheese, or margarine containers, or milk cartons. If you have a patio or yard, use a bushel basket, a wooden box, a five-gallon plastic trash can, a pail, an old dishpan, or a laundry basket lined with plastic sheeting.

Remember that all plants need drainage, so make sure you provide drainage holes or place a layer of gravel on the bottom.

Prepare the soil

The Department of Agriculture recommends for indoor vegetable gardens a synthetic prepared soil that is available at garden-supply centers. It is a mixture of vermiculite, peat moss, and fertilizers, and is sterile and lightweight. Of course you can always mix your own soil, combining two parts loam, one part humus or peat moss, and one part coarse sand or perlite, essential for drainage and aeration.

Select the seeds

For minifarms it is best to use the seeds of miniature vegetables. Send away for a seed catalogue and order those that appeal to you. The W. Atlee Burpee Seed Company has a particularly good selection of miniature vegetable seeds; write for a free catalogue to the Burpee office in Philadelphia, Pennsylvania, 19132; Clinton, Iowa, 52732; or Riverside, California, 92502. Some of the vegetables you might wish to try are:

Dwarf Morden Cabbage—produces four-inch heads that are sweet and tender and small enough for close planting.

Minnesota Midget Cantaloupe—three-foot vines produce surprising number of four-inch melons in about sixty days.

Tiny Sweet Carrot—produces three-inch carrots.

Cherokee Cucumber—vines grow to only three feet and produce seven-inch cucumbers in sixty days.

Morden Midget Eggplant—small bushy plants bear medium-sized fruit.

Tiny Tim Tomato—ideal for window gardens, these plants also do well as hanging plants. They are colorful and productive.

Golden Midget Sweet Corn—produces four-inch ears on thirty-inch plants in sixty days.

Tom Thumb Head Lettuce—thrives in window boxes. Lettuce heads are the size of tennis balls.

Mighty Midget Peas—three and a half-inch pods grow on six-inch vines.

Yellow Lollipop Watermelon—three-pound melons have yellow flesh and thin rinds.

Vegetables that are naturally midget-sized, such as radishes, chives, and parsley, are also excellent for minifarms. To make a decorative garden, try flowering kale, which has bright red and green leaves, or Ruby variety lettuce, which has ruffled red leaves. The fernlike tops of carrots and red-veined leaves of beets also make an effective display.

All seed packets are stamped on the back with the year they were produced. Old seeds germinate poorly and are a bad bargain when space is limited, so make sure yours are new.

Most vegetables grow better in full sun than in shade, but they all have slightly different needs, so choose your vegetables according to the amount of sun you can give them.

Cucumbers, peppers, tomatoes, and squash need the most sun. Radishes, carrots, beets, and other root vegetables can stand some shade. Leafy vegetables—lettuce, mustard greens, chives, kale, parsley, swiss chard, and most herbs—do well in partial shade, or on window sills.

Sow your seeds

It is easiest to start seeds in small containers and transplant them to larger pots when they have sprouted. You may start seeds indoors and move them outdoors later.

Start your plants in small aluminum baking pans, plastic trays, plastic egg cartons, or milk cartons. Choose shallow containers to make transplanting easier. Make sure to wash containers thoroughly with hot soapy water before using them. Don't forget to punch holes for drainage.

It is a good idea to label your container with the date and the kind of seed you are planting in it; even an experienced gardener has trouble telling young seedlings apart! To avoid confusion, put only one kind of seed in each container.

There are two ways of planting your flats.

The Traditional Way

Equipment:
1. Synthetic soil or sandy potting soil.
2. A shallow container provided with drainage.
3. Seeds.
4. Labels, written on paper to be taped to the container or written on popsicle sticks to be inserted in the soil.

Method:
1. Label the container and fill it with moist soil.
2. Sprinkle the seeds over the surface of the container. The number of seeds you sow depends on both the size of the seed and the size of the container: the larger the seed, the fewer you should sow. Don't worry about spacing the seeds; it is easier to thin their ranks after they have sprouted.
3. Cover the seeds with soil, and moisten.
4. If the seeds look crowded when they come up, gently pull out or cut off the smaller, weaker ones.

The Convenient Way

Equipment:
1. Peat pellets, available at garden-supply centers. These pellets contain synthetic soil that swells when water is added. They are easy to handle and to transplant.
2. Labels, written on paper to be taped on to the container.
3. A tray or shallow container.
4. A pencil.
5. Seeds.
6. A small amount of peat moss, sand, or soil.

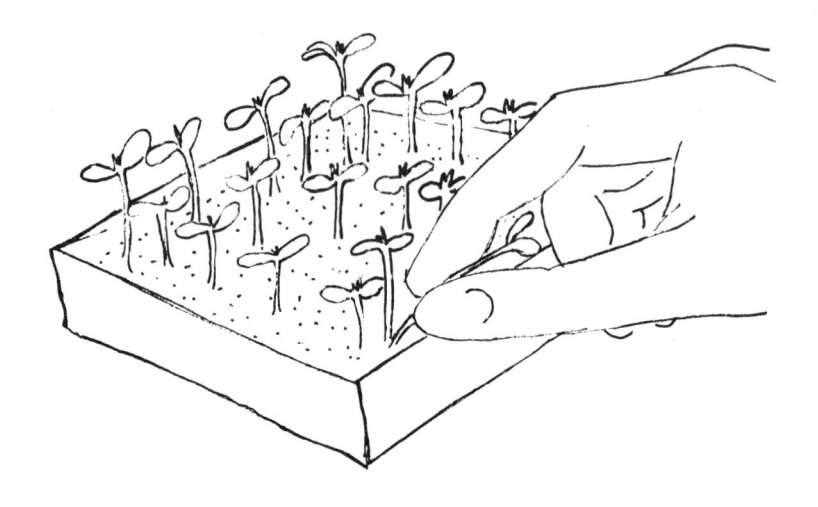

How to thin out seedlings in an overcrowded flat.

Method:
1. Place the pellets side by side in the tray or shallow container. Label the container.
2. Add water until the pellets have swollen and will hold no more.
3. If the pellets do not have holes already prepared, poke holes in them with the pencil. Make deep holes for large seeds like watermelon seeds, and small holes for small seeds like radish seeds.
4. Put two or three seeds in each hole and cover them with a little peat moss, sand, or soil.
5. Moisten slightly.
6. If more than one seedling comes up, gently pull out or snip off the smaller one.

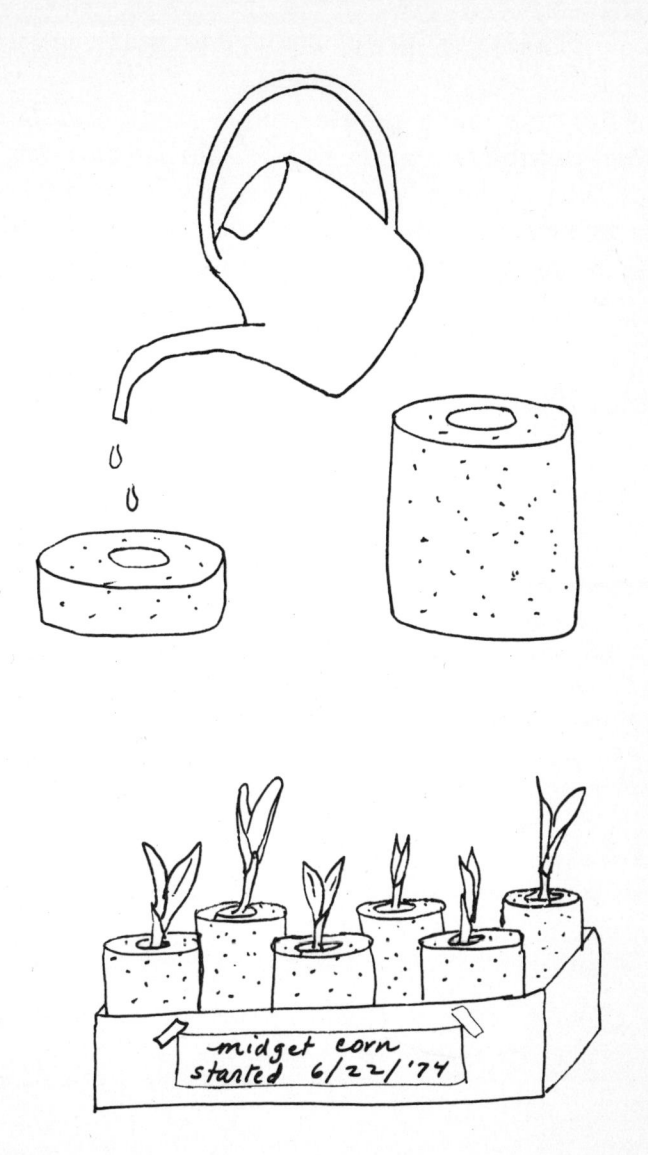

Growing corn in peat pellets. The pellets expand when water is added; then they can be placed in a container and sown with seeds.

68   COMPLETE BOOK OF FLOWERPOT ECOLOGY

After you have planted your seeds and labeled them, put the container in a plastic bag and close the end with a wire twist or rubber band. Once the plants have sprouted, you can remove the plastic bag and move the container to a sunny spot.

Press in the soil around a newly transplanted seedling.

COMPLETE BOOK OF FLOWERPOT ECOLOGY

Transplant the seedlings

When the first two true leaves are fully developed, the plants are ready to be transplanted. Seedlings grown in pellets are easy to transplant: Simply lift out the pellet and set it in a hole dug in the soil of the new pot. Then water. The procedure for seedlings grown in the traditional method is a little trickier:

    a. Lift the seedling carefully out of the flat, taking care not to injure or tear the roots. A popsicle stick makes this easy by providing leverage. Try to keep as much soil as you can intact around the roots. It is easier to preserve the soil ball when it is moist.

    b. Set the seedling into a hole dug in the soil of the new pot or container.

    c. Cover it to stem level and tamp the soil gently around it so that the soil is firm but not packed.

    d. Water the plant to settle the soil around the roots. Check to make sure that the water is draining out of the drainage holes you have provided.

Care for your minifarm

Besides sunlight, plants need only two things: water and fertilizer. If these needs are met, and if you keep a sharp eye out for insect pests, you and your children should produce a bumper crop.

A five-ten-five fertilizer is best for most vegetables. There are many fertilizers on the market, so check the proportions before buying. Apply the fertilizer for the first time three weeks after the true leaves appear, and then at two- to three-week intervals. Follow the directions on the label and follow these basic rules: (1) never feed a dry plant; (2) never feed a sick plant; (3) never overfeed.

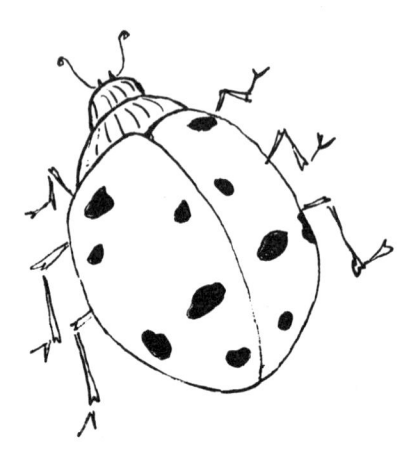

A ladybug.

Watering is a tricky business. Children, especially, are liable to get so excited about their gardens that they literally water them to death. The rule for most plants is do not water them if they still feel wet. Poke your finger an inch into the soil: if it feels dry and crumbly it is time to water. If you have good drainage, water the plants until you see water seeping out the bottom. Do not let the pots stand in water, however; the plants will get "wet feet," which causes root rot. Try not to wet the leaves if you water in the evening because wet leaves in the dark are susceptible to fungus growth. It is safest to water in the morning and on bright days, when the water can evaporate quickly if the leaves get wet.

Insecticides and children are a dangerous combination; if your plants become hopelessly infested, it is better to throw them out than risk using chemical controls. In any case, a thorough washing under a spray of plain water will wash away most bugs. A bulb spray or watering can filled with warm soapy water is also often effective. Try putting large plants right under the shower. Rinse off soap with clear water. If you find any ladybugs outdoors, bring one home and set it in your minifarm. It will protect your plants from any tiny insects that might try to invade your terrain.

7. Harvest your minivegetables when they are ripe. *Bon appetit!*

SOME QUESTIONS AND ANSWERS ABOUT MINIVEGETABLE GARDENING

Why should you use two or three seeds in a pot when you only want one plant to grow?

Commercial seeds are tested by the seed companies for the percentage that will germinate at a given time, and the package is stamped with the rate. If it says eighty percent germination, eighty seeds out of a hundred will germinate. But you have no way of knowing if you are planting one of the twenty that will not, so it is a good idea to play it safe by planting extra seeds.

What is five-ten-five fertilizer and why is it necessary?

Plants need fifteen different elements to be vigorous and to produce fruit and seeds. Three of those elements, oxygen, carbon, and hydrogen, come from the air and from the water in the soil; the other twelve must come from the soil. Of these twelve, the three most likely to be lacking are nitrogen, phosphorus, and potassium. Chemical fertilizers therefore contain these three elements, always listed in that order. A well-balanced fertilizer is based on a ratio of one percent nitrogen, two percent phosphorus, and one percent potassium or potash. Five-ten-five means that the fertilizer has five percent nitrogen, ten percent phosphorus, and five percent potassium, which is the correct one-two-one ratio.

The nitrogen is necessary for the production of leaves and stems. Too much nitrogen retards the production of flowers and fruits and produces overly dense foliage. Phosphorus is important in the production of flowers, fruits, and seeds. Potassium promotes root growth, improves the general health of the plant, and increases its resistance to disease.

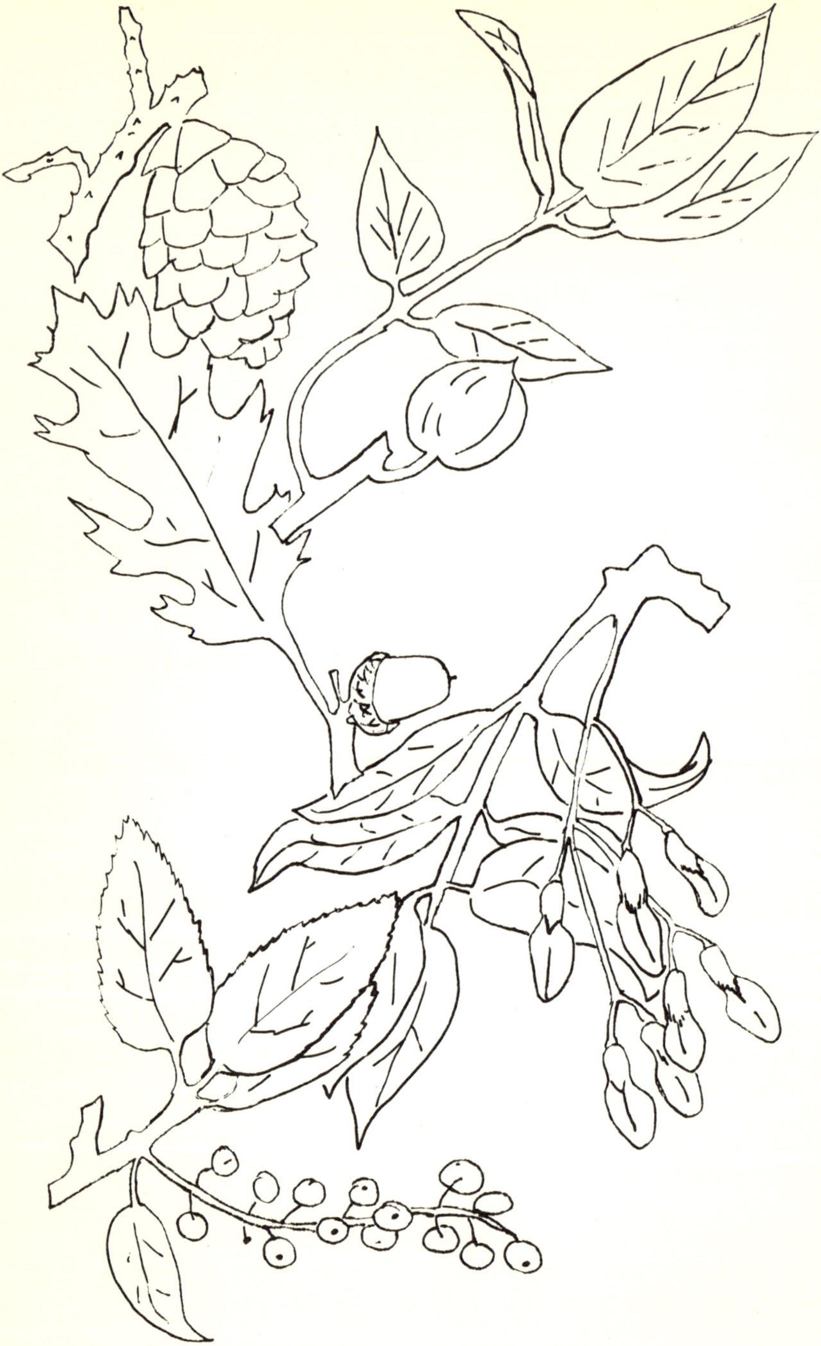

Chapter III

Miniforests: Finding Out How Mighty Oaks from Little Acorns Grow

It is great fun for children to walk through the woods in autumn looking for berries and nuts that contain seeds suitable for planting, but they can also find these treasures in city parks or on tree-lined streets. Most children already know the winged fruit of the maple and the nuts of the oak and horse chestnut, and they can be taught to recognize other, more unusual kinds of tree seeds as well.

Some tree seeds to collect and grow in a miniforest. The trees and seeds shown are, from top to bottom, red spruce, pignut hickory, red oak, white ash, and black cherry.

All species of trees produce seeds after flowering, although often the flowers are small, green, and very inconspicuous. Locust, catalpa, or Kentucky coffee tree seeds are hidden in pods; maple, ash, or ailanthus seeds have wings to carry them in the wind; the beech, walnut, and hickory seeds are enclosed in a hard case; wild cherry, sassafras, and hackberry seeds are in berries; and evergreen conifer seeds are neatly tucked in the scales of cones.

To start a miniature forest, conduct a seed hunt (see Project 1) and gather as many seeds as possible. The best time to go seed hunting is in the fall, when the fruits of most trees are ripe. If you prefer to go seed hunting in late spring or early summer, look for the early-ripening fruit of the elm and silver or red maple. You will find the fruit and seeds of a tree around its base or among the leaves. Remember that the fruit is likely to be near the ends of the twigs, because that is where the current year's growth is.

Occasionally you will find trees with no fruits. These may be too young to bear fruit, or, like the red oak, they may take two years to produce fruit, or they may be male trees of a species that has male flowers on some trees and female flowers on others. Some of the most common trees—willows, poplars, and ginkgoes—have separate sexes; if you wish to try growing one of these "dioecious" trees, you must look for fruit on a female tree. The only way to tell male and female trees apart is by the flowers. The females are the ones with the fruit. Like any other seeds, tree seeds are suitable for planting. Trees with small leaves will look prettiest in miniforests.

How to start your forest:
Gather a number of seeds, putting each kind in a separate bag. You will have to look inside the cones of evergreens to find the seeds; shake the cone well and the seeds will fall out. Some tree seeds can be planted directly, others will need special treatment.

Separate the seeds according to the treatment they require.

Seeds that require no special treatment: These are spring-ripening seeds such as the poplar, magnolia, elm and red or silver maple, and the seeds of subtropical trees, mangroves and palms, for instance. Simply plant the seeds in a shallow tray of moist sand, vermiculite, or a mixture of the two. If there are wings or other seed-dispersal apparatus, remove them before planting the seeds. Plant at least ten seeds of each type to ensure success.

Seeds that need soaking to soften the seed coats: These include most seeds that grow in beanlike pods, such as the Kentucky coffee tree, honey locust, black locust, California redbud, acacia, and mesquite. Remove the seeds from the pods and soak them until they seem softened. Then plant as above.

Seeds that require cold, moist treatment: These include most northern trees such as alders, ashes, basswoods, beeches, birches, horse chestnuts, apples, pears, plums, cherries, firs, hemlocks, sassafras, white pines, sweetgums, sycamores, and maples other than red or silver. Seeds of these trees may be planted in the fall in moist sand and kept in a cold place over the winter. In the spring they will germinate and produce healthy seedlings. However, if more immediate results are desired, we have had great success simulating winter by putting the seeds in water in ice cube trays and allowing them to stay frozen for two or three weeks. After they have been frozen in this way, they can be planted in a moist medium and kept in a warm spot. If they are kept moist and warm, they should germinate.

Transplant the seedlings

When the seedlings have developed their second set of leaves, put them in two-inch pots or paper cups filled with a mixture of potting soil and sand or perlite.

Maple and pine seedlings potted in paper cups.

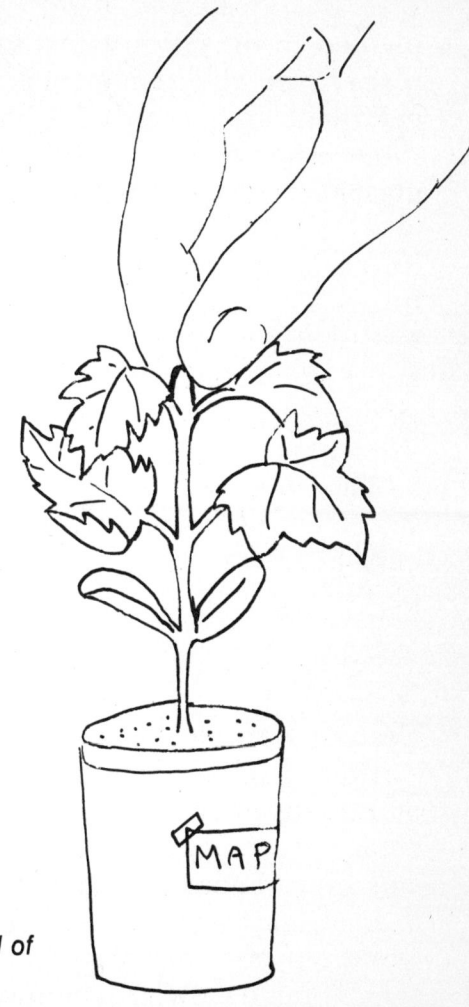

Pinching off the terminal bud of a seedling maple.

To keep your trees miniature, pinch off the terminal buds (the end buds) when the seedlings are four or five inches tall. Pinching will keep the plants at about that height. If roots appear through the drainage holes, cut them off.

A Japanese miniforest landscape.

Design a forest landscape

After the plants have been in small pots for about a month, decide how you wish to arrange them. Your choice of arrangement will depend partly on the size and appearance of the container you use. As long as it is at least two inches deep, any container will work, but minitrees will do best in porous containers. Wooden bowls, window boxes, and unglazed clay dishes are ideal. If possible, make drainage holes in the bottom of the container you choose. Be sure, in any case, to provide for adequate drainage by placing a layer of pebbles on the bottom. To discourage bacteria, add a few small pieces of charcoal. You may want to plant a group of one

COMPLETE BOOK OF FLOWERPOT ECOLOGY

species together or create a landscape with different species. To grow a miniorchard, use apples, pears, cherries, or plums. Or you can design a pine forest or a Japanese garden. If you choose to make a Japanese garden, use an odd number of plants and make a tiny path of pebbles or pine needles between groupings of miniature trees.

Before transplanting minitrees, water them; this helps keep the soil intact around the roots. Then turn the minitrees out of their pots by holding them upside down in one hand, with your fingers spread over the top to support the plant, and sharply tapping the bottom of the pot with a trowel or other instrument held in the other hand. Next, dig holes in the soil of the new container, set in the minitrees, and press the soil in around them. The plants should be far enough apart so their leaves do not touch.

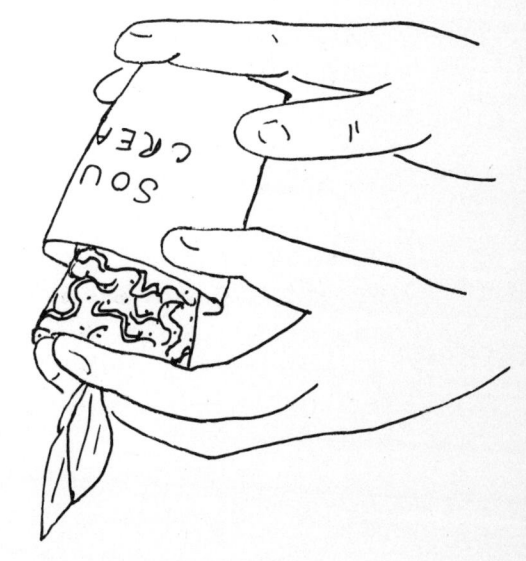

How to turn a plant out of its pot.

Care for your forest garden

Frequent pruning by pinching off the terminal buds on the branches makes the plants more compact. Since the terminal bud is the growing tip of the plant, removing it will cause dormant buds lower on the stem to develop. Pruning also dwarfs the size of the leaves by depriving them of some nourishment; this improves the plant's proportions. In general, prune before new growth has reached one inch.

If you have deciduous trees (plants that lose all their leaves at one time in the autumn), they should go into a cold environment for the winter. Put them on a sheltered terrace, porch, or window ledge, or in an unheated garage, and water only very slightly every two weeks. In the spring water them thoroughly, fertilize them with a mild fertilizer, and watch the buds open.

The care of your miniature forest involves the same procedures as the care of other plants, but because the roots of the trees may fill the dish or container, water frequently and add mild fertilizer every two weeks. Covering the soil with a layer of moss helps keep the soil moist.

Result: Your miniforest, with adequate drainage and fertilizing, will last indefinitely.

SOME QUESTIONS AND ANSWERS ABOUT TREES

Why is it necessary to gather many seeds of each species?

In the north only about fifty percent of the seeds found will produce hardy seedlings. The viability of seeds varies from about ten percent for aspens, birches, and elms to almost one hundred percent for oaks and walnuts.

Do evergreens keep their needles without ever losing them?

Evergreens shed their leaves—or needles—but only gradually, unlike deciduous trees, which lose all their leaves annually.

How will you recognize the seedlings in a miniforest?

In general seedling leaves have the same shape as the leaves of mature trees. Therefore, as soon as they develop their true leaves, in a matter of weeks, the seedlings are recognizable. If you do not know how to tell trees apart, get a tree guide. We like *Trees of North America* by C. Frank Brockman (Golden Press: 1968), but there are many others.

You may prefer to label the seeds when you plant them. If so, simply follow the labeling procedures for minifarms.

Can you transplant minitrees outdoors?

Any time you tire of a miniforest, you can plant it

outdoors. The minitrees have not been damaged by dwarfing, and will develop readily into full-sized trees.

Do all trees lend themselves equally well to dwarfing?
All trees can be dwarfed, but trees with naturally small leaves are better proportioned for miniforests and will work best. Although such a large-leafed tree as the horse chestnut or catalpa will grow in a miniforest, it will look out of place.

What is the difference between a tree and a shrub? Will a shrub grow in a miniforest?
A tree has one main stem or trunk; a shrub has several stems growing up from the roots. Shrubs are usually smaller than trees.
Some shrubs lend themselves very well to dwarfing. Azaleas, junipers, jasmine, quince, heather, yews, and cotoneasters are shrubs that look particularly pretty in miniforests. The dwarfing procedures for shrubs are the same as those for trees.

PART TWO
REPRODUCING PLANTS WITHOUT SEEDS

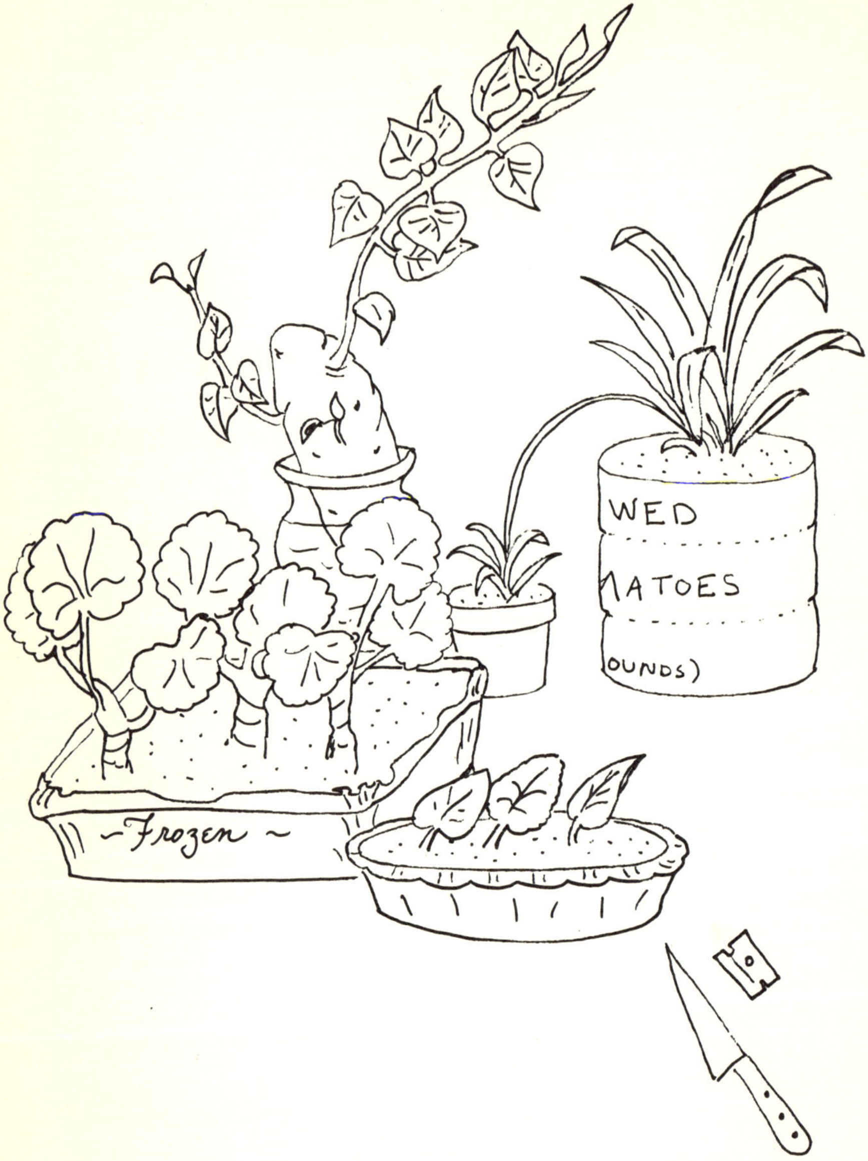
WED
ATOES
OUNDS)
-Frozen-

Chapter IV
New Plants from Old Stems

Many plants can reproduce without seeds, through what is called vegetative or asexual reproduction. This process is carried on widely in nature and explains, for example, how water hyacinths, which reproduce by sending out underground stems, can quickly cover a wide pond. It is estimated that ten water hyacinths could produce 655,360 new plants in eight months by vegetative reproduction. Although most flowering plants produce seeds, vegetative reproduction provides another—sometimes more efficient—method.

Man has learned from nature and artificially carries on vegetative propagation of many food crops: apples, avocados, bananas, citrus fruits, dates, figs, pineapples, pears, and potatoes. Artificial propagation simply involves separating a part of a plant from the parent plant; almost any part is capable of producing roots and developing into a new plant.

All the descendants of a single parent plant that are produced in this way are called a clone. All McIntosh apple trees, for example, are members of a clone: They are the descendants of a seedling discovered in Ontario by John McIntosh, who recognized the plant's superlative characteristics, nurtured it, and made cuttings from it. All name varieties of any plant—grapes, carnations, geraniums, potatoes, or whatever—are members of a clone and were produced by vegetative propagation.

There are many advantages to this method of propagation. First, you know exactly what the offspring will be like: They will be identical to the parent. Second, you can start with a fully developed plant, instead of waiting for seeds to grow. Finally, some plants do not produce seeds, and the only way they can multiply is by vegetative means. This is true of such widely cultivated plants as pineapples, navel oranges, bananas, and some limes.

COMPLETE BOOK OF FLOWERPOT ECOLOGY

PROJECTS

1. *A Trading Slips Club (stem tip cuttings)*

One of the easiest and most common ways to propagate plants without seeds is by means of stem tip cuttings. Stem tip cuttings are also the most common way to share plants with friends. A group of children might start a "trading-plants" club, collecting cuttings (sometimes called "slips") from parents, friends, and neighbors, growing them, and trading new cuttings with each other. Since taking cuttings is actually good for most plants, plant lovers

Making a stem tip cutting from a wandering jew. The cut is made below the node—the place where a leaf comes out of the stem.

are generous with them, and it is easy to build a large collection of plants from cuttings without spending a penny.

Novice cutting collectors will have the best luck with freely branching plants, such as wandering jew, coleus, geranium, begonia, fuchsia, nasturtiums, and impatiens.

Since taking cuttings involves both dexterity and the use of a sharp knife, this project is not recommended for children under eight years old.

Equipment:
1. A sharp knife or single-edge razor blade for cutting—not scissors. Scissors, because they cut with a squeezing action, may bruise the base of a cut stem and prevent it from healing properly.
2. Root-forming hormone such as Rootone, Stimroot, or Proliferol (optional). These are available inexpensively in nurseries or in hardware or five-and-ten-cent stores and are not poisonous or dangerous to children.
3. A container deep enough to hold the cutting inserted to a depth of two inches. Don't forget to provide for drainage.
4. Rooting medium: coarse sand, bird gravel, perlite, or vermiculite, alone or mixed with peat moss.
5. A plastic bag.
6. A fork.

Method:
1. Carefully choose your cutting. Select a stalk that has not flowered and is still green. Avoid stalks with the largest leaves; they wilt easily. Make your cuttings early in the day when the plant tissue is firm and crisp, especially if the plant is outdoors.

2. Using a sharp knife or single-edge razor, make the cut about a half inch below a node—the place where a leaf comes out of the stem. The growing tissue of a plant is located at the nodes, and that is where new roots will develop.
3. The cutting should be about three or four inches long and contain at least two nodes.
4. Strip the leaves from the bottom of the stem.
5. (Optional) Dip the end of the cutting in a root-inducing hormone, following the manufacturer's directions. To avoid contaminating the whole packet of hormone, shake a little of the powder onto a piece of paper, dip the end of the cutting into the powder, and then shake off the excess.

Geranium cuttings inserted in rooting medium.

6. Moisten the medium, make a hole in it for the cutting with a pencil or your finger, and insert the cutting. Cuttings should be just deep enough to be secure, and the medium should be pressed firmly around them. If you are starting several cuttings in the same container, discourage mold by leaving enough room between them so that the leaves do not touch and all can receive light. Make sure, too, that none of the leaves touches the soil.

A miniature greenhouse made with a plastic bag and wire coat hangers twisted into arches.

7. After the cuttings are securely inserted, water again so that the medium is washed tightly against the cutting but is not soggy.
8. Cover the container with thin plastic to maintain humidity. If you use a small container, such as a paper cup, simply slip it into a plastic bag and close the top. For a larger container, make a miniature greenhouse: Twist wire coat hangers into arches, stand them in each end of the container, and cover the whole thing with clear plastic. The plastic bags that cleaners use work well: Just slip the container inside and fasten the ends together with a wire twist or rubber band. If too much moisture collects inside the bag, remove it, turn it inside out, dry the outside, and replace it.
9. Place the container in good light but away from direct sunlight. Examine the cuttings periodically for mold, and remove dead leaves. If you see signs of mold or mildew, remove the affected parts and open the plastic bag slightly to allow more ventilation.
10. After two weeks, carefully dig up a cutting with a kitchen fork to see if rooting has begun. If you don't see new roots, press the cutting back into the medium. If rooting has started, begin to leave the cover off a little longer each day. Begin by leaving the end of the plastic bag open for two days. Each day after that, roll back the plastic an inch more until you remove it entirely.
11. When there are a number of roots about an inch long, the cuttings are ready to be transplanted to pots. This should be in about four weeks.

Results: With regular watering and fertilizing, the cutting will grow into a vigorous plant.

Propagating a spider plant. The plantlet is still connected to the parent by a runner.

COMPLETE BOOK OF FLOWERPOT ECOLOGY   95

2. *Stolon Fruits (runners or stolons)*

Some plants are especially easy to propagate because they send out runners or stolons. These are really stems, but where they touch the soil they will produce roots and send up shoots. Houseplants that produce runners, such as the spider plant, are simple to root and grow.

Equipment:
   1. A "parent" spider plant or strawberry geranium with developed runners.
   2. A small container filled with moistened soil.
   3. A hairpin.

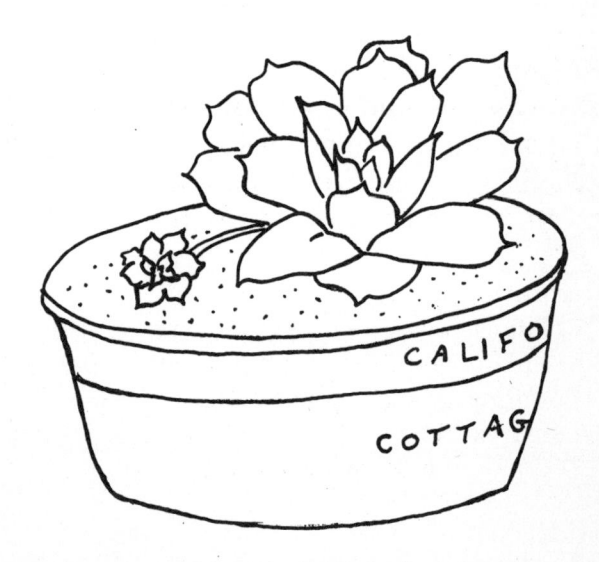

Hen and chickens. The "chicken" offset is connected to the "hen" by a short runner.

Method:
1. Place the small container near the "parent" plant and put the little plantlet at the end of the runner on the soil, anchoring it with the hairpin.
2. When the plantlet has developed roots, usually in just a few days, cut the cord that connects it to the "parent." You now have a viable new plant.

Sometimes runners are very short (in that case they are called "offsets") and cannot be rooted in a separate pot while connected to the "parent." *Sempervivum*, commonly called "houseleek" or "hen-and-chickens," is one of these. The offsets—in this case "chickens"—of plants of this kind can be broken off and rooted as cuttings.

3. Rhizome Rearing (underground stems)

Rhizomes are underground stems. Just like upright stems, they have nodes (or joints), and at these nodes side buds and roots may grow. When these buds develop, you have a new plant.

Equipment:
1. A Chinese evergreen (*Aglaonema*), ginger root, cast iron plant *(Aspidistra)*, philodendron, pothos, lily of the valley, or snake plant (Sansevieria).
2. A sharp knife.
3. A container filled with rooting medium.

Method:
1. Cut the rhizome so that the piece you remove to root has a growth bud or "eye." You can cut one rhizome into several pieces, but be sure each piece has an "eye."

How to take a cutting from a snake plant.

2. Place the piece of rhizome on the rooting medium so that the dormant eye comes in contact with it. Press the cutting in place but do not cover it.
3. When roots have formed, the cutting is ready to be potted.

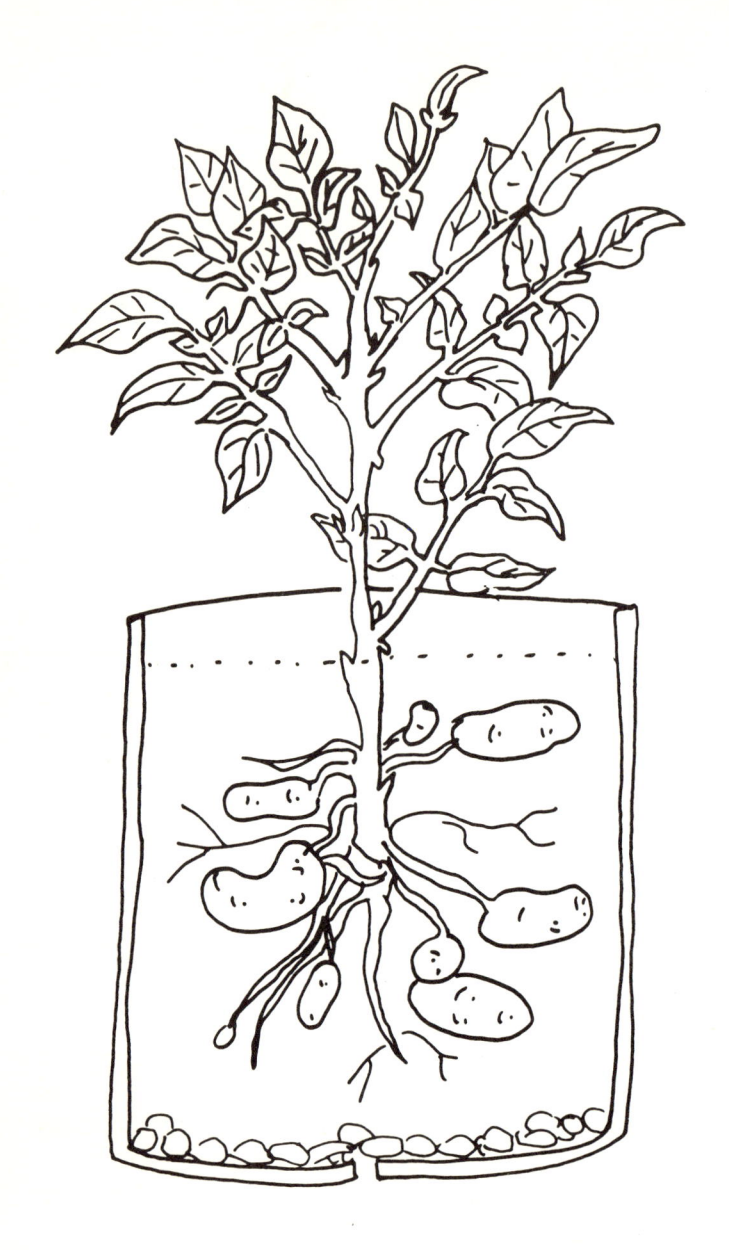

A potato plant ready for harvesting.

4. A Potato Patch (tubers)

An underground stem that is round and large with stored food is called a tuber. The ordinary white potato is the most familiar example. You probably have seen sprouts growing out of the eyes of old potatoes kept in a warm place. If you remember that the potato is really a stem, you can recognize the eye as a bud. A new plant can be started from any piece of the tuber that has an eye.

Equipment:
1. A white potato.
2. A knife.
3. A container five or six inches deep filled with soil. A coffee can with holes punched in the bottom would work well.

Method:
1. Cut the potato in sections so that each section has two or three eyes. Leave as much of the potato as possible on each piece to provide stored food for the developing plant.
2. Bury the piece, cut side down, with the eyes facing up, about three inches below the soil.
3. Keep the soil moist. When the shoots start to appear, put the container in good light. Continue regular watering.

Result: Shoots will grow from each "eye" and an attractive potato plant will develop. After it produces flowers it will begin to wither. Then turn it out of the pot and harvest a crop of new potatoes. Look for the shriveled remains of the potato piece you originally planted: It has exhausted itself in supplying food for the new shoots.

Because the potato plant is an annual, once it has produced flowers and seeds and a crop of new potatoes its reproductive function is over, and it dies. If you leave the new potatoes in the soil, however, they will send up new shoots and begin the cycle again.

5. *An Onion Bouquet (bulbs)*

A bulb is an underground stem that is wrapped in fleshy leaves. Onions are typical bulbs: Try cutting one in half longitudinally and examining it. The hard plate at the bottom is the stem and the leaf buds are attached to it. In the very center of the bulb is the flower bud; the fleshy layers around it are leaves that store food. To the side of the flower bud you may notice a smaller bud. This is the bulb bud, which will develop into a new bulb.

Equipment:
1. A firm onion, unpeeled.
2. A jar of water.
3. Toothpicks.

Cross section of an onion, showing the flower bud in the center, the smaller bulb bud on the left, the storage leaves surrounding the buds, and the short stem at the bottom.

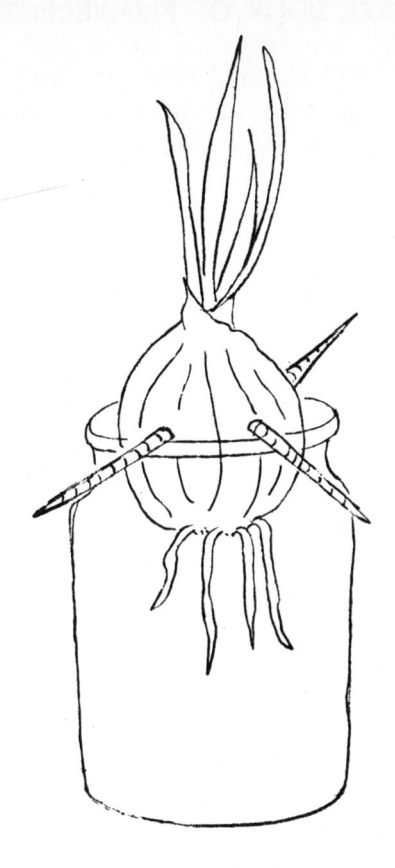

Growing an onion in water.

Method:
1. Place the onion on top of the jar of water so that the flat end is submerged. If the onion is too small, support it with three toothpicks set in around the middle. Make sure the bottom touches the water.
2. Keep the onion out of the light and watch the root system develop. In a few days, when roots have grown about two inches, move the onion to the sun

and watch the shoot grow. You may even get a flower. By this time the bulb will have exhausted itself and will shrivel.

Result: Your onion bouquet will be interesting, despite its strong onion fragrance.

6. *April in February (forcing bulbs)*

To enjoy spring in winter, try forcing some flowering bulbs. When you "force" a bulb, you compel it to change its normal growing pattern. Normally bulbs winter in the ground and blossom in the spring; when they are planted in pots and encouraged to root and flower indoors in the winter, ahead of their natural schedule, they are being "forced."

Forcing takes its toll on bulbs. By blooming early they use up all their stored energy and cannot blossom again the following year. In nature, on the other hand, a bulb would not only produce a new plant from its flowering bud, it would also produce a new bulb from its bulb bud. Of course, forced flowers, like all others, produce seeds that can be planted, although it would take several years for the seeds to develop into bulbs energetic enough to flower.

Not all bulbs are equally easy to force. Tulips, daffodils, and hyacinths require a complicated process of preconditioning, including at least three months of precooling, and would try the patience of young gardeners. We recommend for children the paper white and *soleil d'or* varieties of narcissus, which are inexpensive, easy to grow, pretty, and

Paper white narcissus in flower.

fragrant. Because their growers have preconditioned them to flower early indoors, they have a very high success rate, and children will see roots begin to form within a few days and blossoms in two or three weeks.

Equipment:
1. Three, five, or seven firm, healthy narcissus bulbs (an odd number looks prettier).
2. A container not less than two inches deep. For one bulb an old teacup works well; for several try a shallow baking dish. (Don't use a valuable glass or china container because the minerals and acids that build up in the water may etch or discolor it.)
3. Pebbles, gravel, or perlite.

Method:
1. Fill the container with enough carefully washed pebbles or perlite to anchor the bulbs—about half full.
2. Place the bulbs a half inch apart and a half inch from the rim of the container.
3. Pour in enough water so that the bottom of the bulb is touching the water.
4. Add enough pebbles to cover the bottom third of the bulb.
5. Place the bulbs in a dark, cool place to force root growth. Check every day to make sure the water level is maintained.
6. In about ten days there should be good root growth. When the bulbs have enough roots to be firmly anchored in the pebbles, they are ready to be placed near a window. Give the container a half turn each day, so that the shoots will grow evenly.
7. Add room-temperature water as needed.

Results: In about four weeks the flowers will blossom. In a cool place the flowers will last several weeks. Since forcing will have exhausted the bulbs, discard them when the flowers fade. If you have a backyard, try burying them. Perhaps after a year or two underground they will have accumulated enough strength to bloom again outdoors.

SOME QUESTIONS AND ANSWERS ABOUT STEMS

Can a stem cutting be made at any time from any plant?

A cutting can be made at any time, but it is best to wait until the plant is starting active growth. If the plant is going into a dormant period, the cutting will be slow to root.

Choose only healthy-looking plants for cuttings. The cutting is never healthier than the parent.

You can make stem cuttings from all plants. However, some plants have more hormones than others and will root more easily. Freely branching plants such as coleus and wandering jew are among these. Plants with low natural-hormone levels—the yew, camellia, and holly, for instance—need treatment with a growth-promoting substance to root successfully.

Why are the cuttings made below the node?

In the region of the node there is a concentration of meristematic tissue (rapidly multiplying cells) and consequently the roots will develop most rapidly there.

Can stem cuttings be started in water?
Very often cuttings will root in a glass of water, but the roots become tangled and brittle and are easily broken when they are disentangled. Moreover, it is difficult for roots to make the adjustment from water to soil, so they may suffer a severe setback when the cutting is potted.

Why do onions and potatoes begin to shrivel when they sprout?
The food stored in the fleshy leaves of the onion and in the stem of the potato begins to be used up by the plant as it grows.

How can you recognize a healthy bulb?
The bulb should be large and firm; it should show no sprouts and be without splits.

Can bulbs that have been forced to flower be used again next year?
No. They would have to spend several years under ground outdoors before they can again store up enough energy to bloom.

What is root hormone?
Root hormone contains indolebutyric acid, indoleacetic acid, naphthaleneacetic acid, and minute quantities of more than thirty other chemicals. Although cuttings will root without it, root hormone greatly promotes growth.

An experiment comparing the rates of growth of cuttings untreated and those treated with hormone would be interesting for older children. To do this experiment, make twelve cuttings from a coleus. Treat six with root hormone and leave the others untreated. Label containers "treated" and "untreated," note the date, and insert the cuttings into the appropriate containers. Keep all the cuttings under identical conditions. After three days gently dig up one treated cutting and one untreated cutting, measure root growth, and record your findings. Do this five more times at three-day intervals, using the remaining cuttings. Then compare results.

Can you grow more potatoes from the seeds produced by the plants in the potato patch project?
Like all flowering plants, potato plants will grow from seeds. But since the eye of the potato has a great deal more stored food available to it than the tiny potato seed, it will grow more quickly and more vigorously. Even if your potato seeds do sprout, they will only produce small tubers. Commercial growers never raise crop potatoes from seed.

If your onion plant flowers, can you grow a new onion from its seeds?
It is always possible to grow new plants from seeds. However, onion seeds germinate very slowly and are not hardy, so you could not be sure of success. Commercial growers use seeds for hybridizing purposes, but usually propagate onions from offsets of the bulbs.

QUICK-FROZEN
~LASAGNA~

Chapter V
Stirring Dull Roots

Like stems and leaves, roots vary widely in form and function. Fibrous roots, which are slender and threadlike, and storage or tap roots, which are thick and fleshy, are the two basic kinds of roots that develop from the plant embryo. Some kinds of plants also have adventitious roots, which grow from leaves or stems. The main function of roots is to take in water and minerals to sustain the plant, but certain types of roots can also be used for anchorage, storing food, climbing, and—of interest to us here—propagation.

PROJECTS

1. Root Division

Probably the easiest way for an amateur to increase his supply of plants is by root division. Many plants form buds at the base of old stems. After a while these buds develop into new shoots. When house plants begin to send up such shoots, they can simply be turned out of their pots and separated. Often they will divide easily and naturally.

The best time to do this is in late winter or early spring, just as new growth is beginning.

Equipment:
1. An African violet, *Sansevieria*, strawberry begonia, fern, or any plant that seems to have baby plants around the mother plant.
2. Two forks.
3. Pots filled with damp soil and provided with adequate drainage.

Method:
1. Turn the plant out of its pot by holding it upside down in one hand, with your fingers spread over the top to support the plant, and sharply tapping the bottom of the pot with a trowel or other instrument held in the other hand.
2. Using the two forks back to back, gently separate the newer shoot, taking care to disturb the roots as little as possible.
3. Pot the divided plants, but do not add additional water for two or three days. Keep the plants out of bright sunlight for a week to prevent excessive loss of water from the leaves before the root hairs develop. The root hairs are the chief water-absorbing organs of the plant.

Dividing the roots of a Calathea with forks.

2. A Sweet Potato Vine

The most familiar examples of storage roots are the root vegetables, which are rich in energy. Carrots, sweet potatoes, beets, turnips, radishes, and parsnips are all storage roots. One way that they are different from many other plants is that they are biennials. This means that it takes them two years to produce seeds. When the seeds are planted, the root and then the shoot grow. As the leaves carry on photosynthesis—the process by which plants make food—the excess food is stored in the root, and the root becomes plump. If the root is left in the ground over the winter, its stored energy will be used the following spring to send up new shoots that will flower and produce seeds. By that time the food stored in the root will be completely used up.

Unlike white potatoes, which are underground stems, sweet potatoes are storage roots. But they too will grow into interesting plants.

Equipment:
1. A carefully selected sweet potato. Choose a plump old one that shows signs of sprouts so you know it will grow. Many sweet potatoes have been treated with a growth inhibitor or covered with wax to keep them from sprouting in the market. If they have been freshly dug, they won't sprout either, since they need a rest period. Best results are obtained with old potatoes.
2. A widemouthed glass jar or tumbler, almost filled with water.

Method:
1. Place the potato in the jar with the pointed end in the water. The top of the jar should be small enough

Growing a sweet potato in water.

so that only the bottom half of the potato is in the water. If the opening is too large, stick three toothpicks into the potato to support it on the edge of the jar.
2. Keep the potato out of the light until the fibrous roots appear. Check frequently to make sure the water level is maintained in the jar.
3. When the fibrous roots have developed, move the potato to the light and watch the shoots grow.
4. Pick off the weaker shoots, leaving only two or three of the stronger ones.
5. When a good root system has developed, you can plant the whole potato in a pot of soil and keep it well watered. If you prefer, you can keep it in water.

Result: The potato will sprout a fast-growing attractive vine with red stems and bright green leaves. The vine can be tied up with strings to frame a window, or it can be allowed to trail from a hanging basket. Since the sweet potato will continue to function as a storage root, accumulating excess food produced by the leaves, it will not shrivel, and will last indefinitely indoors. Under sunny conditions you may even get pretty clusters of flowers.

A sweet potato vine framing a window.

A carrot top growing in sand.

3. *A Carrot and Beet Garden*

Many of the other familiar storage roots—carrots, radishes, beets, turnips, and parsnips—can also quickly produce interesting plants. These roots can be cultivated individually, or combined for variety; the fernlike leaves of carrots and the dark green and purple-red foliage of beets look particularly striking together. The procedures for cultivating all these plants are the same.

Equipment:
1. A fat carrot (and/or beet or other storage root).
2. A shallow container.
3. A rooting medium: either coarse sand, peat moss, perlite, or pebbles.
4. A knife.

Method:
1. Cut off any old leaves that may still be on the carrot, leaving one half to one inch of leaf stubble.
2. Cut the carrot or beet in two, horizontally about one and a half inches below the top.
3. Fill the container with the sand, peat moss, perlite, or pebble rooting medium to within a half inch of the top.
4. Leaving the top exposed, push the carrot or beet down into the growing medium.
5. Add just enough water to make the medium moist, and place the container in a sunny spot.
6. As the leaves begin to grow, increase the amount of water.

Result: Within a week lovely foliage will start to appear. Add mild liquid fertilizer every two weeks, and the foliage will last indefinitely. It is very unlikely, though not impossible, that a carrot top grown indoors in rooting medium will have enough energy to blossom. If you are lucky and get a flower, save the seeds to grow the next year.

4. *A Carrot Hanging Basket*

Storage roots such as carrots can also be made into pretty hanging baskets. If you have fun making a carrot basket, try the same procedure with a beet,

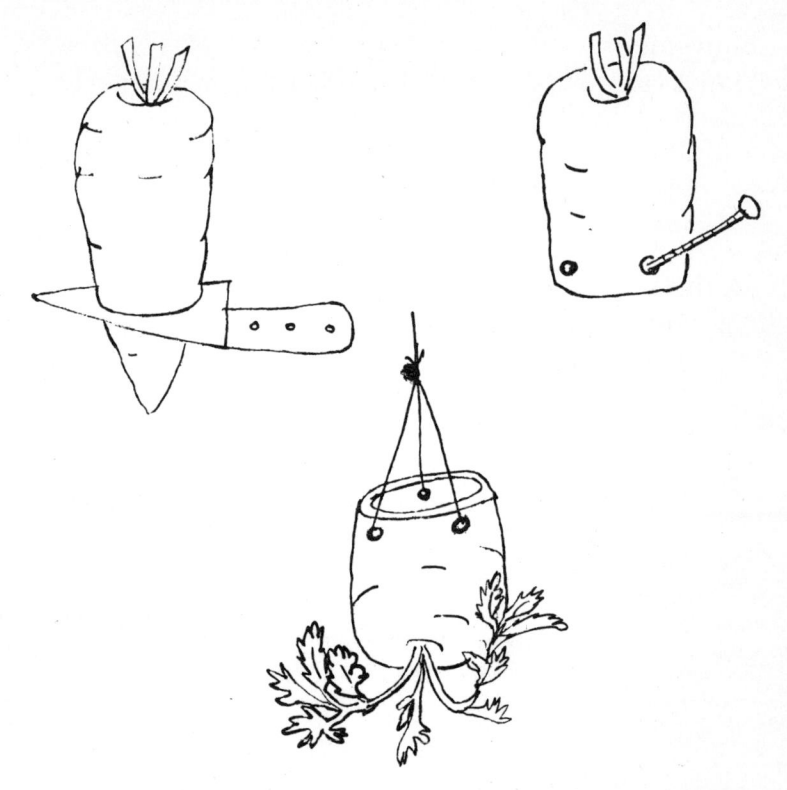

How to make a carrot-hanging basked: Cut off the bottom of the carrot (as shown in the upper left), make three equidistant holes with a nail (as shown in the upper right), and hollow out the center. The completed carrot basket is shown at the bottom; notice that the leaves are beginning to grow upward against the pull of gravity.

parsnip, or turnip. This project is worthwhile not only because it teaches children about roots, but also because it demonstrates geotropism—the ability of plants to know which end is up.

Younger children should not try this project, which calls for the use of a knife and an apple corer.

Equipment:
1. A plump carrot.
2. A slender nail.
3. A knife.
4. An apple corer.
5. Three lengths of string, wire, or raffia, eight to ten inches long.

Method:
1. If any leaves are left on the carrot, cut them off.
2. Cut off the bottom tip, or pointed end, of the carrot about one and a half inches from the bottom.
3. About one-half inch above where you have cut off the bottom, make three holes with the nail. They should go through to the center core and be about equidistant because they will be used to hang the "basket."
4. Hollow out the center of the cut end of the carrot with the apple corer. Be careful not to cut through to the outside of the carrot.
5. Thread one end of each length of wire or string through one of each of the three holes and firmly knot it. Then tie the three free ends firmly together. Now the basket is hanging so that the carrot is upside down.
6. Fill the center cavity with water and keep it filled.
7. Hang the upside-down carrot in good light.

Result: Soon the fernlike leaves will start to grow. Then they will turn up and eventually cover the "basket."

SOME QUESTIONS AND ANSWERS ABOUT ROOTS

How are the fibrous roots that grow out of the propagated storage roots different from the storage roots themselves?

The function of fibrous roots is to absorb moisture and nutrients from the soil. They branch freely and are slender and threadlike. Storage roots, as the name implies, are storehouses of nourishment. They thicken as the plant accumulates food. Just as some animals store excess food as fat, so some plants can store excess food in their roots.

Why should the weaker shoots be picked off a sprouting storage root?

If you pick off some of the weaker shoots, all the stored energy in the storage root can be used by the stronger ones so they will develop rapidly into healthy plants.

Will sweet potato vines eventually produce new sweet potatoes?

Under ideal conditions the sweet potato root will throw off an offshoot or "draw," which can be separated from the parent root to start a new plant. This is the method commercial growers use.

Propagation from seeds produced by the flowers is slow, since it takes time for a fleshy root as large as the sweet potato to develop. It is faster to propagate sweet potatoes by taking stem tip cuttings from the vines; see Chapter IV, Project 1 on page 89 to find out how this is done.

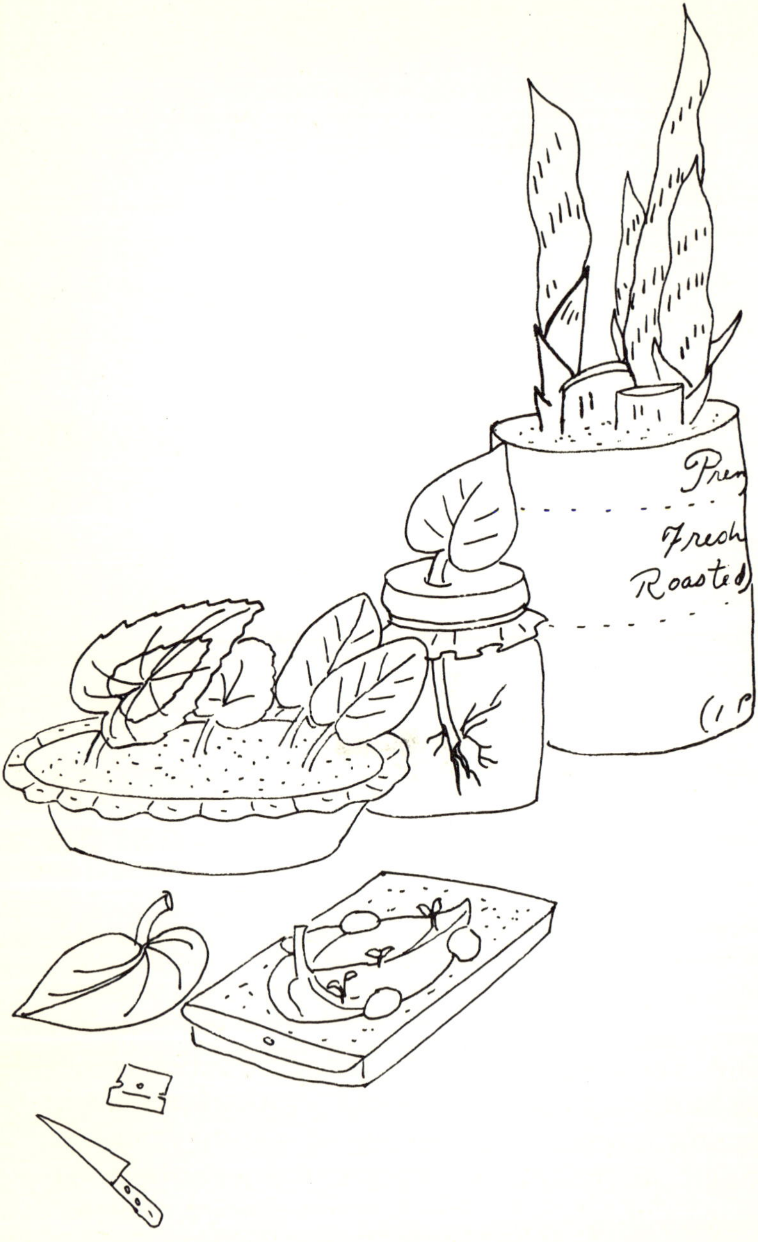
Fresh
Roasted

Chapter VI
Turning Over a New Leaf

New plants can be made from leaves or pieces of leaves of some plants. Plants with thick leaves, such as African violets, begonias, peperomias, and *Sansevieria* lend themselves particularly well to this method of propagation.

There are several methods for starting leaf cuttings. Whatever method you use, make your cutting in the same way: Choose a healthy leaf, and with a sharp knife cut it from the base of the parent plant. The leaf should have a stalk or petiole about one inch long. Dip the cut end in rooting hormone to promote growth. Since taking leaf cuttings requires using a sharp knife, we suggest that an adult make the incisions; the children can take over from there.

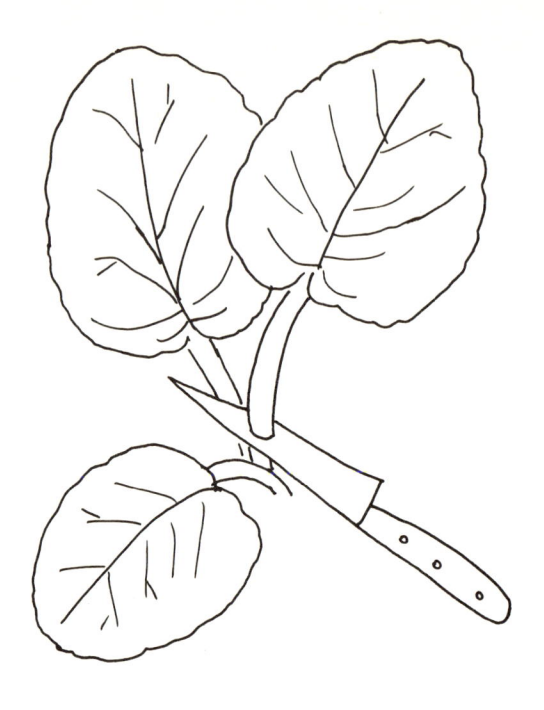

How to cut a leaf from its parent plant.

PROJECTS

1. *Starting Leaf Cuttings in Soil*

Equipment:
    1. A cut leaf dipped in rooting hormone.
    2. Soil, one-third sand and two-thirds peat moss.
    3. Sand or perlite to use as rooting medium.
    4. A small container provided with drainage.

Method:
1. Fill the container with soil up to two inches from the top. Add a one and a half inch layer of sand or perlite as a rooting medium.
2. Set the leaf in the rooting medium on a slant so that a small part of the leaf blade is also covered.
3. Water thoroughly and continue to keep moist, but not soggy.

Result: The roots will grow slowly through the rooting medium into the soil, so no repotting will be necessary.

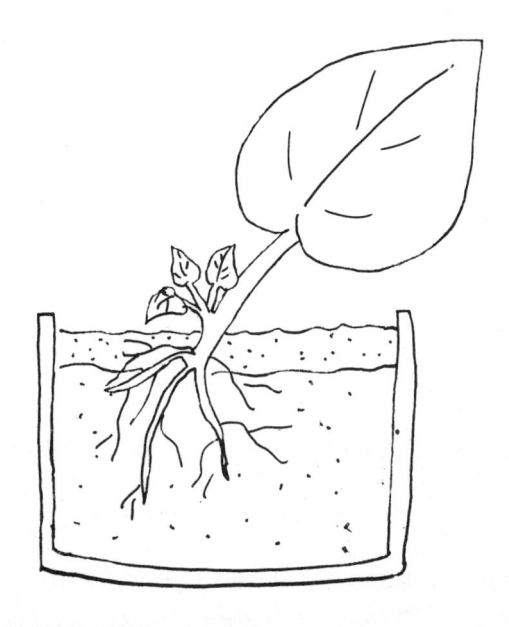

Propagating an African violet leaf in soil.

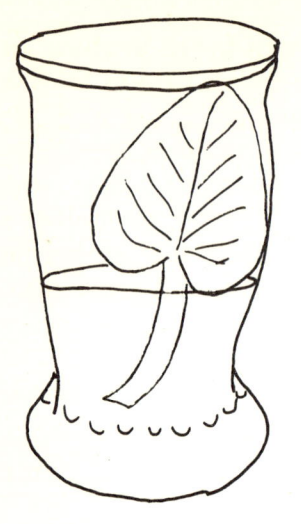

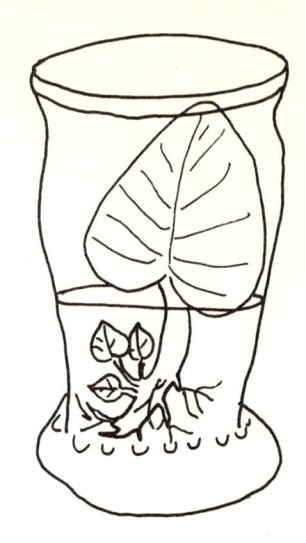

An African violet leaf propagating in water. The leaf on the right has developed a plantlet and is ready for potting.

2. Two Ways to Start Leaf Cuttings in Water

The Plain Way

Equipment:
1. A small, narrow glass (the type cheese spread comes in) half-filled with water.
2. A healthy leaf dipped in rooting hormone.
3. A small container filled with a mixture of one-third sand and two-thirds damp peat moss.

Method:
1. Rest the leaf against the inside of the glass so that only the stem is in water. Place the glass in a bright spot out of direct sunlight and check it regularly to make sure the water has not evaporated.

COMPLETE BOOK OF FLOWERPOT ECOLOGY   125

2. In about four weeks roots will begin to show and small plantlets will appear at the base of the leaf. When the roots are one-quarter to one-half inch long, pot the cutting in the mixture of vermiculite and damp peat moss.
3. After the small plantlets have grown an inch or so tall, carefully separate them from the mother leaf and pot them individually. Each will grow into a new plant.

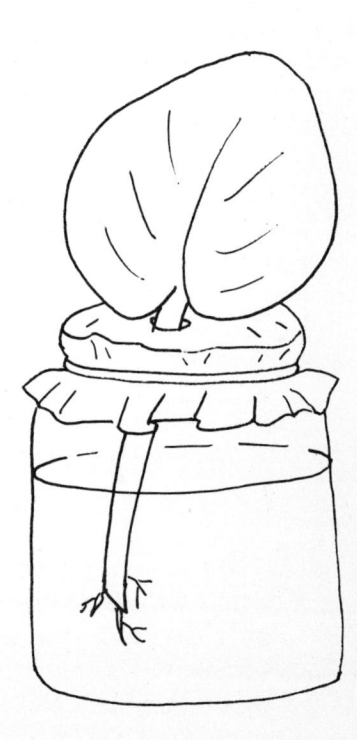

Rooting a leaf in water the fancy way.

The Fancy Way

Equipment:
1. A drinking glass or glass jar.
2. A piece of plastic wrap.
3. A rubber band.
4. A pencil.
5. A healthy leaf dipped in rooting hormone.
6. A small container filled with a mixture of one-third sand or vermiculite and two-thirds damp peat moss.

Method:
1. Fill the glass with water.
2. Cover it tightly with plastic wrap secured with the rubber band.
3. Poke a small hole with the pencil in the center of the plastic wrap.
4. Push the stalk of the leaf through the hole so that it is submerged in the water and the leaf blade remains out.
5. When roots show, pot the cutting as described above.

The advantage of this method is that the water in the glass does not evaporate; however, it is a little tricky to set up.

3. Bits That Grow Big

Plants may be propagated by using pieces of leaves, as this, and the following two projects show.

Equipment:
1. A shallow container filled with rooting medium, preferably coarse sand.
2. A healthy leaf from a *Sansevieria* or snake plant.
3. A knife.

How to propagate snake plants from pieces of leaves: Each leaf bit, after being inserted in rooting medium, will develop one or more plantlets.

Method:
1. Cut the leaf horizontally on a slant in two-inch long pieces. Be sure to mark the top of each piece so you don't plant it upside down. Small children will need help with this step.
2. Allow the pieces to rest for several days in a dry place. Because these leaves are fleshy they can subsist on stored food and water.
3. Set the pieces upright, bottom side down, in the rooting medium. Moisten the medium and keep the cuttings in a cool place.
4. When roots of about one inch have formed, the cuttings are ready to be potted in sandy soil.

4. Triangles

Wax and semperflorens begonias, which are popular as houseplants and as ornamental edgings in parks and malls, can be propagated easily from triangular bits of leaves. While this project would work for many other kinds of plants, we recommend these begonias because they are easy to come by and quick to show results. Small children will need help cutting their triangles.

Equipment:
1. A large, fully developed leaf from a wax or semperflorens begonia.
2. A sharp knife.
3. A cutting board.
4. A shallow container filled with damp sand.
5. A clear plastic or glass bowl.

Method:
1. Place the leaf face down on the cutting board and cut a triangle in the center. The apex of your triangle should be at the stem end and should intersect with the largest vein.

How to make a triangular begonia leaf cutting: Cut a triangular piece from a leaf; as shown at the upper left, and insert it, apex down, in rooting medium, as shown on the right. The plantlet develops where the vein has been inserted in the medium.

2. Discard the stem and outer edge of the leaf, retaining only the triangle.
3. Insert the triangle so it is upright with the apex down in the damp sand.
4. Cover the container with the plastic or glass bowl.
5. Keep it in a light spot but away from direct sunlight.

Result: In about two weeks a new plant will begin to develop from the large vein, and the triangle will start to disintegrate. When the new plant is two to three inches tall, pot it in soil.

5. *In the Same Vein—an Instant Begonia Garden*

There are many types of begonias. Those with very large leaf veins, such as the angel-wing and rex begonias, do best at breeding from bits.

We suggest using begonias for growing from bits because we have had the most success with them. Theoretically any large-veined leaf will work, but for various reasons most other varieties do not root as readily as the begonia.

The cutting required in this project is simple, but keep an eye on younger children if they want to do it themselves.

Equipment:
1. A large, fleshy leaf from an angel-wing or rex begonia.
2. A sharp knife.
3. A cutting board.
4. A shallow container filled with damp sand, vermiculite, or perlite.
5. A few pebbles.
6. A clear glass or plastic bowl.

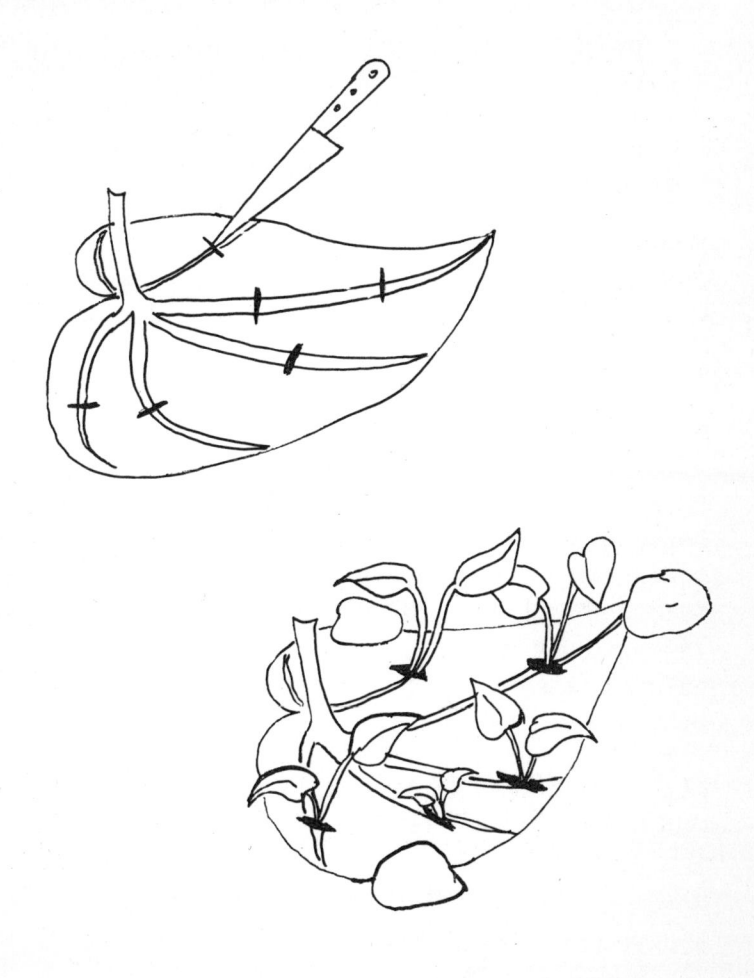

How to grow new plants at the veins of a begonia leaf: First, nick the veins with a knife. Then anchor the leaf with pebbles face down on rooting medium and watch the plantlets grow.

Method:
1. Put the leaf face down on the cutting board. With the knife, make a knick in each vein. Your cut should go about halfway through the vein. Do not sever it.
2. Turn the leaf over and lay it, face up, on the damp sand, perlite, or vermiculite, so that the cut veins are down.
3. Place a few pebbles around the edges of the leaf to keep it flat.
4. Invert the bowl over the container to maintain humidity.
5. Place the container in a light place but away from direct sunlight.

Result: After a few weeks a new plant will grow at each place the vein was cut. When the new plants are two or three inches tall, the mother leaf will have disintegrated and the new plants can be potted individually in soil.

SOME QUESTIONS AND ANSWERS ABOUT LEAF CUTTINGS

Why do some cuttings need to rest before being placed in a rooting medium?
 Cuttings made from succulent plants like the *Sansevieria* need to be allowed to dry out to form a callus. Fresh cuttings are likely to rot and the callus acts as protection. If you are not sure if a callus has formed, set the cutting in a dry medium and water lightly after a few days.

Is it better to start leaf cuttings in water or in rooting medium?

Success is more assured with rooting medium. Some plants will never root in water. Often bacteria develop in water and cause cuttings to rot. Moreover, roots grown in water are thicker and more succulent than those produced in a soil mixture, and may have trouble establishing themselves when the cuttings are potted in soil.

Some plants, such as Chinese evergreen, wandering jew, coleus, pothos, and *Philodendron*, however, will root easily in water.

Why do the new plants in Projects 4 and 5 grow only at the veins of the leaf bits?

Meristematic tissue, which is made up of rapidly multiplying cells, is located in the veins of leaves. There are also concentrations of meristematic tissue at leaf nodes, root tips, and in buds. Plant growth occurs in meristematic tissue.

PART THREE
PLANTS AND
THEIR COMMUNITIES

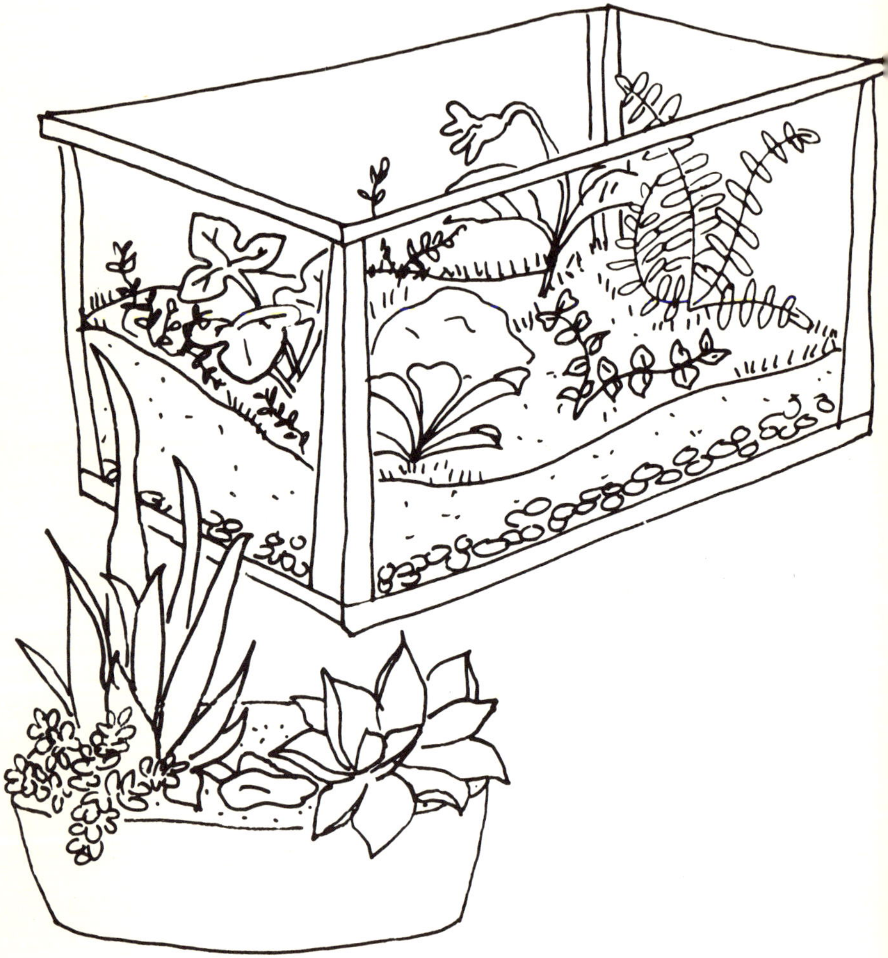

Chapter VII
Ecosystems

An ecosystem is a community of plants and animals together with nonliving material. The basis of an ecosystem is cooperation. The nonliving environment supplies minerals, air, and water. Green plants make food for themselves, other plants, and animals, and provide oxygen. Dead plants and animals, acted upon by fungi and bacteria, contribute chemical elements to renew the cycle of life. Ideally an ecosystem is balanced and self-sufficient: All its parts interact to sustain life.

Children can recreate ecosystems at home or in the classroom by constructing terraria. A terrarium is more than a pretty glass garden: It is a miniature habitat that can even support a very small animal.

Although the terraria currently sold as decorative items often contain a hodgepodge of plants, a good terrarium—one that will both look attractive and last—must make sense ecologically. It must be planned as an ecosystem, a complete natural environment.

PROJECTS
1. Building a terrarium case

A terrarium can be any size from a small jar, clear plastic box, or brandy snifter to a large discarded aquarium, but the easiest to plant and maintain are rectangular and straight-sided. It is fun for older children to build their own terrarium cases. The one described in this project is eight by eight by ten inches with a cover that lifts with a little tab.

Equipment:
1. Glass, one-eighth-inch thick (ordinary window glass). Have the hardware store cut the glass in six pieces:
    Four pieces—eight inches by ten inches
    Two pieces—eight inches by seven and three-quarter inches
2. Cloth, plastic or nylon adhesive tape, five and one-third yards long, one inch wide. Green tape is desirable.

Method:
1. Cut the adhesive tape as follows:
    Two strips ten inches long
    Four strips eight inches long
    Two strips seven and three-quarter inches long
These strips will hold the container together.
Then cut:
    One strip three inches long
    Two strips eight inches long
    One strip nine and three-quarter inches long
    Two strips ten inches long.
These strips are for the cover of the terrarium.

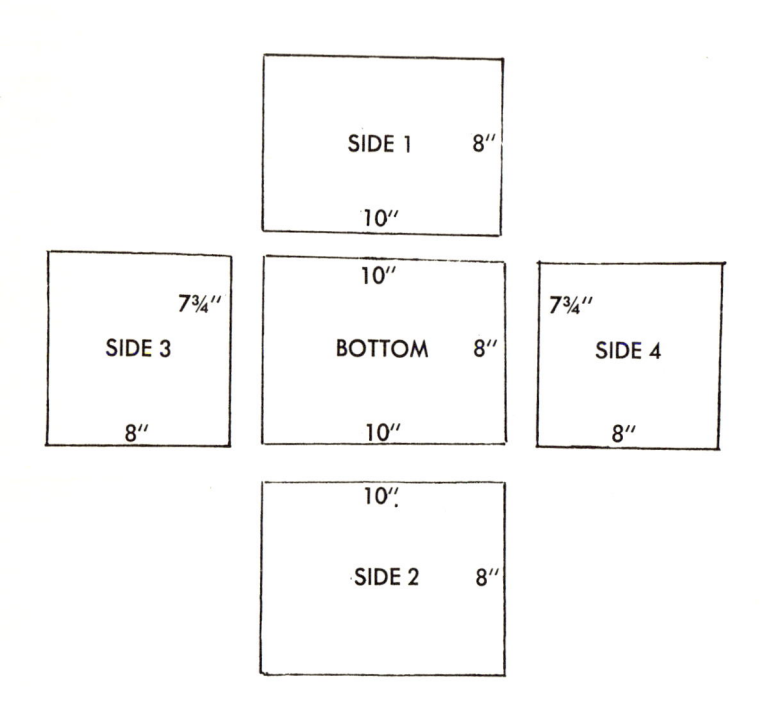

	SIDE 1 8″	
	10″	
7¾″ SIDE 3 8″	10″ BOTTOM 8″ 10″	7¾″ SIDE 4 8″
	10″ SIDE 2 8″	

How to arrange the pieces of glass for a terrarium case.

2. Draw a faint pencil line down the center of each piece of tape to guide you in placing the tape. Then put the strips aside along with one eight-by-ten inch pane of glass.
3. Arrange the five pieces of glass that will form the bottom and sides of the container into a cross, as in the diagram. The eight-by-ten inch piece that goes in the center will be the bottom; the four other pieces that form the arms of the cross will be the sides. Leave a space between the pieces equal to the thickness of the glass.
4. Using the ten-inch strips of tape, fasten sides 1 and 2 (the ten-inch sides) to the bottom.

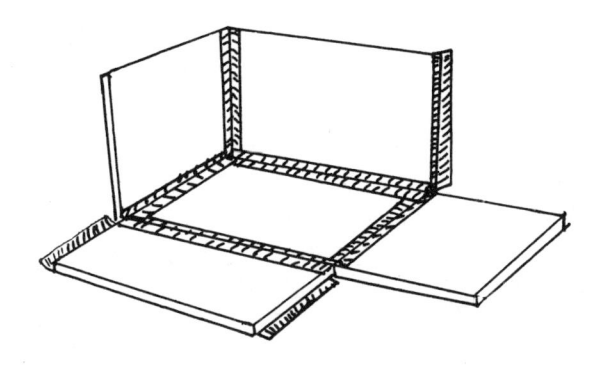

Sides 1 and 4 of the terrarium case are shown after they have been raised and attached with tape. Sides 2 and 3 are now ready to be raised and attached with the free edges of the tape.

5. Using the seven and three-quarter-inch strips of tape, fasten sides 3 and 4 (the seven and three-quarter-inch sides) to the bottom. Rub the tape very firmly on the glass to make a permanent attachment.
6. Using four of the eight-inch strips of tape, fasten strips to the eight-inch sides of sides 1 and 2, leaving one-half inch of the tape extending free the whole length of each side.
7. Carefully pick up the five attached pieces and turn them over.
8. Raise sides 1 and 4, and holding them firmly in place on the bottom glass, attach the free edge of the tape on side 1 to side 4. Now raise side 2 and in the same way attach the free edge of tape on side 1. Repeat the process with side 3. Be sure that each side rests on the bottom piece of glass. Now the case should stand by itself.
9. The next step is to strengthen the bottom. Decide which side of the case will be the back. Starting at the center of the back, extend a piece of tape all around the bottom, fastening one-half inch of the tape to the sides and leaving one-half inch free. Carefully pinch the tape together at the corners. Cut the corners, and fold in the free half of the tape against the bottom, pressing firmly. Bind the top edge in the same way, for reinforcement.
10. Now make the cover. Bind the eight-inch sides with the two strips of eight-inch tape. Next attach one end of the three-inch piece of tape to the middle of a ten-inch side, fold it back on itself, and attach the other end to the underside of the glass. This will be used as a tab to lift the cover. To complete the cover, take a ten-inch strip of tape and, through its center, make a one-inch longitudinal slit. Pull the tab through this slit, then bind the tape to the glass.

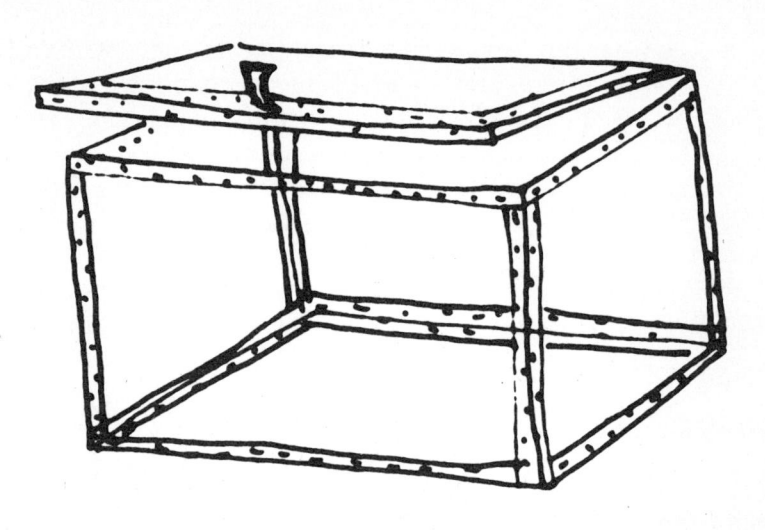

The completed terrarium case, with a cover that lifts with a little tab.

11. Fasten the cover to the terrarium by attaching the other ten-inch side to the back, using the ten-inch strip of tape on the outside of the glass and the nine and three-quarter inch strip on the inside.
12. To seal up any cracks or spaces in the corners of the terrarium case, you may want to use spackling compound, which you can buy inexpensively at any hardware or paint-supply store. Just pour in the spackle to a depth of three-eighths inch and allow it to set overnight.
13. If you were not able to buy green tape, you can color the tape you used with a green crayon.

Result: Your glass box will be sturdy, attractive, and watertight—ideal for a terrarium.

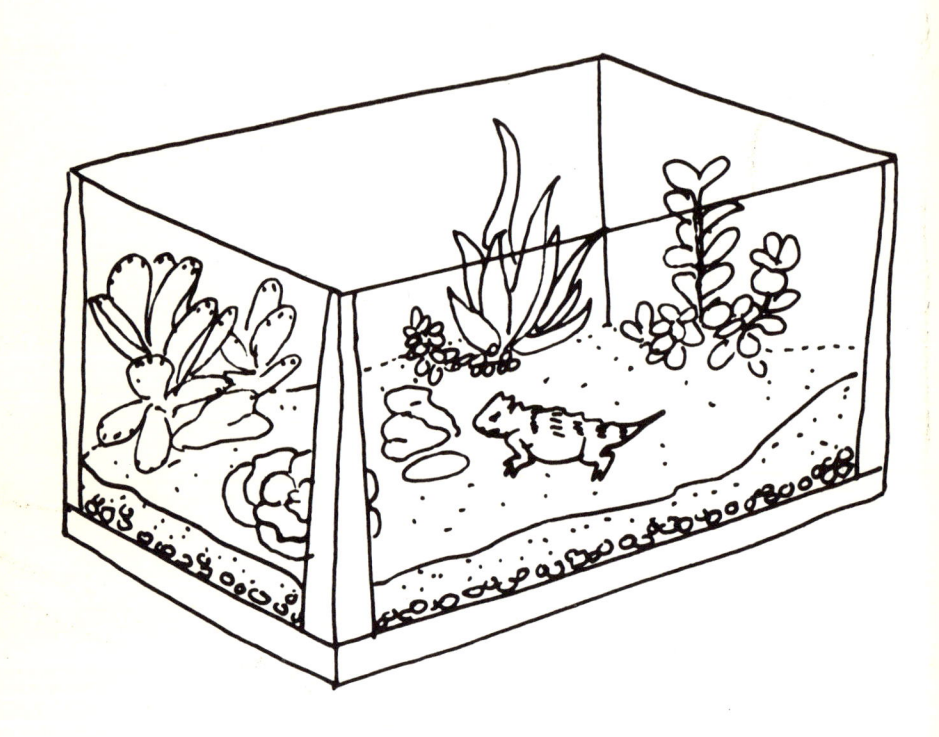

A desert terrarium inhabited by a collared lizard. It is planted, from left to right, with Crassula hemisphaerica, Kalenhoe tomentosa *(panda-plant)*, Sedum pachyphyllum *(jelly-bean plant)*, Crassula schmidtii, *and* Adromischus maculatus.

2. A Desert Terrarium

This type of terrarium is perhaps the easiest to assemble and maintain.

Equipment:
1. A clean terrarium case.
2. Pebbles.
3. Coarse sand, available where aquaria are sold.
4. Sandy potting soil (cactus mix).
5. Fine white or light-colored sand.
6. A collection of tiny potted cacti or other succulents (plants with fleshy leaves or stems), such as cardinal's cap, jelly-bean plant, old man aloe, burro-tail, *Stapeliad,* hen-and-chickens, and *Kalenchoe.* Spiny cactus should be avoided, especially if you are working with young children. If you prefer, grow your plants from stem or leaf cuttings, as described in the projects in Part Two of this book. Insert the cuttings right in your desert terrarium and they will root easily. You can also grow desert plants from seeds, but this takes longer. Send away to Burpee or any other seed company for a catalogue. (See Appendix B.)
7. (Optional) A horned toad or collared lizard, available at pet stores. If you buy an animal, at the same time buy meal worms to feed it. Once you have two dozen mealworms, they will propagate themselves easily. You can also catch insects for your animals.
8. (Optional) Some decorative stones.

Method:
1. All terraria need drainage and aeration. Supply this by covering the bottom of the case with a one-inch layer of gravel or pebbles, followed by a one-inch layer of coarse sand.

2. Cover the drainage material with two to four inches of sandy potting soil, slightly moistened. Shape the soil to resemble a rolling landscape, making miniature hills and valleys. Add a few pretty stones for interest.
3. Spread a one-half inch layer of the fine sand over the top.
4. Now use the plants to plan the landscape. You may remove the plants from their pots, but it is easier just to bury the tiny pots in the sand. These pots are sufficient because desert plants in a terrarium have enough water and do not need to spread their roots in search of more. Place the larger plants in back, the shorter plants in front. If you're using prickly cacti, wear thick gloves. Plants should hever touch the glass, which gets very hot and may burn the leaves .
5. Little desert animals make the scene more realistic. If you use them, be sure the cover is escape-proof. Be sure also to provide them with drinking water. Burying a small plastic container of water in the sand will create a natural-looking watering hole. Drop in two or three mealworms a day from your supply for food. Terrarium animals eat very little.
6. To care for this desert community, keep it in a warm, sunny location, 68° to 80° F. Spray water on the soil around the plants once a week, taking care not to wet the plants themselves. If an animal is kept in the terrarium, check its drinking water.

3. *A Woodland Terrarium*

Woodland terraria are probably the prettiest and most popular. Although the materials for them can also be purchased, it is most fun to make them from small plants collected in the woods. Even in the city, mosses and ferns grow in shaded moist corners, and

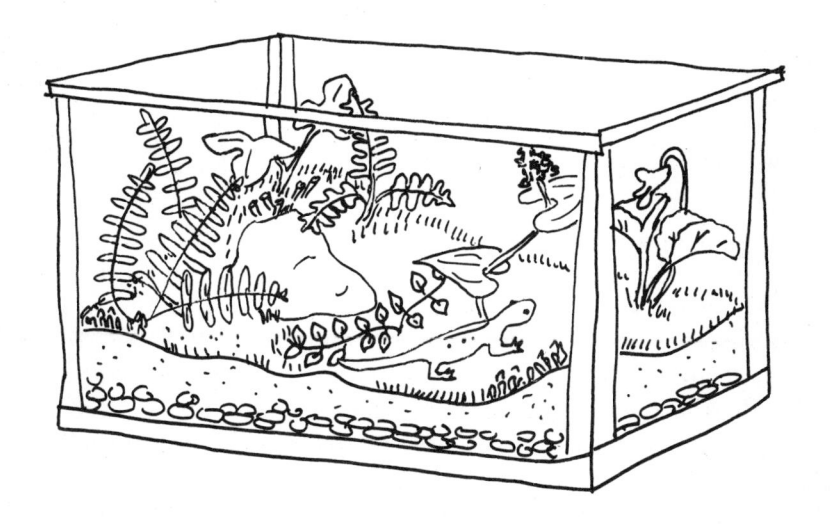

A woodland terrarium inhabited by a newt and planted with ferns, mosses, and wildflowers.

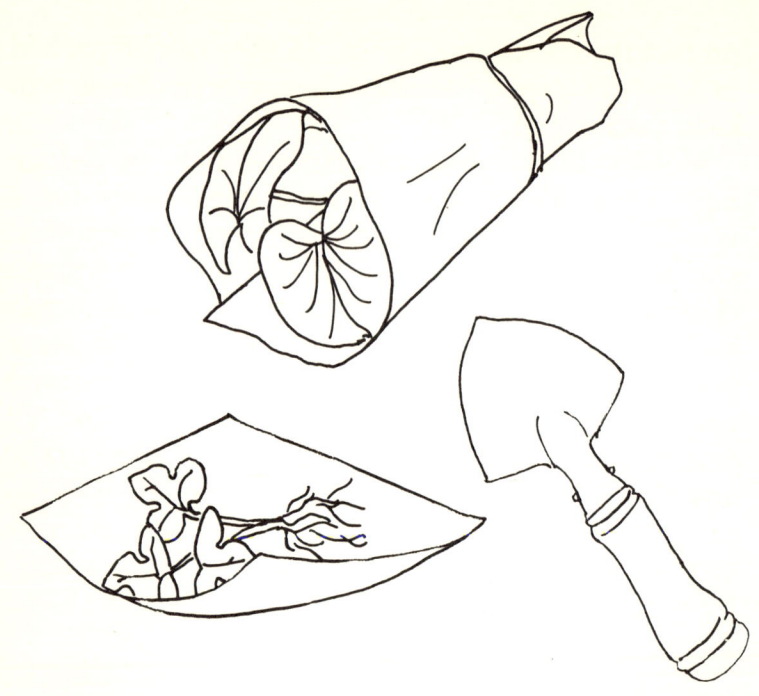

Woodland plants wrapped in paper to protect leaves and stems.

a collecting expedition is an ideal way for children to begin to study ecology. Be sure, if you are doing your own collecting, to get permission from the owner of the land you are exploring.

Collectors should go armed with trowels or little shovels, newspaper, and plastic bags. Try to plan a collecting expedition for the fall; plants collected then, after the ideal growing conditions of the summer, do particularly well. Dig each plant carefully, keeping the soil surrounding the roots, and wrap it in paper, making a funnel or collar to

COMPLETE BOOK OF FLOWERPOT ECOLOGY 149

protect the stems and leaves. Mosses can be packed in layers of paper. Storing specimens in plastic will keep them moist.

Mosses, liverworts, club mosses, lichens, *Selaginella*, and wood ferns make a good basis for a woodland community. Little seedlings of hemlock, spruce, laurel, and juniper are evergeen, and make charming miniature forests. Little oak and maple seedlings offer variety in color and texture. Much of the fun of collecting your own terrarium material comes from the unexpected plants that spring up from the seeds that were lodged in the soil. Actually any tiny woodland plant will thrive in a terrarium, provided it has been dug up and replanted with its original ball of soil intact.

Equipment:
1. A clean terrarium case.
2. Clean gravel or pebbles.
3. Coarse sand.
4. A few small pieces of charcoal.
5. Sandy garden soil, dampened. If the soil will hold together when squeezed in the hand, it is wet enough.
6. A small bag of leaf mold. Leaf mold, available where garden supplies are sold, is made of decomposing leaves and duplicates the conditions of a woodland environment.
7. A collection of lichen-covered rocks, tiny ferns, seedling trees, moist moss, small hemlock cones, broken pine needles, twigs.
8. (Optional) Small animals such as newts, toads, tree frogs, chameleons, garter snakes and beetles. Animals larger than the newt will need supplementary

feeding with mealworms, available from pet stores, or live insects that you can catch. For small animals, place little pieces of rotting wood in the terrarium. These will contain enough small insects to sustain the animal.

Method:
1. Prepare a two-inch base of gravel and cover it with the coarse sand. Scatter the charcoal and press it into the sand.
2. Cover this drainage material with one to two inches of garden soil.
3. Spread leaf mold over the soil.
4. Plan your landscape. You may build the soil up on the sides or at the back, making hills and valleys. Use the rocks to simulate boulders and ledges. Sink a glass or clear plastic dish into the soil and surround it with pebbles to make a miniature pond.
6. Set in the plants, not too close together, making sure the leaves do not touch the glass. Cover the bare spots with moss and press firmly. Use the hemlock cones, pine needles, and twigs to create a woodsy look.
7. If you wish, put in an animal. Toads and salamanders are easy to find or buy, but they tend to dig up the moss and spoil the terrarium. If you add a chameleon, be sure to provide it with a stiff plant to climb. Snakes and tree frogs are clever at escaping, so if you use one, have a very tight cover. Animals larger than a salamander need to have two or three mealworms added daily for food.
8. After the garden is planted, mist it well with the sprinkler.
9. Clean the glass and cover the terrarium.
10. The terrarium will be easy to maintain. Keep it in good light but out of direct sunlight. Clean the glass

A newt will do well in a woodland or bog terrarium.

periodically and remove any debris or yellowing leaves. If there is a great deal of condensation on the glass in the morning, lift the cover off for an hour. If condensation continues, prop the cover up a crack with a round toothpick. If there is little condensation and the plants look dry, the terrarium needs a spraying. Too much moisture and too much heat cause mold and spindly plant growth. If mold develops, dust the terrarium lightly with powdered sulfur, a harmless substance available in drug or hardware stores. Once the terrarium becomes established, it rarely needs additional care.

A cultivated garden terrarium in a glass candy jar. The ground cover is baby's tears; above are fittonia, on the left, and watermelon peperomia, on the right. A maidenhair fern grows in back.

4. *A Cultivated Garden Terrarium*

In the city it may be difficult to get wild plants, but a cultivated garden terrarium may be just as pretty and almost as interesting. Buy the smallest plants you can; they are least expensive and will thrive in a terrarium. You can be adventurous in choosing a variety of species. Often the very plants that will suffer in the dry air of an overheated apartment will flourish in the constant environment of the terrarium.

In choosing plants, think about creating contrasts in height, color, and texture. Avoid plants that grow very tall, such as *Ficus,* Chinese evergreen or Boston fern; nothing is more pitiful to see than a plant deformed by a cover holding down its head. Choose some creeping plants as ground cover: baby tears, small-leaved episcias, such as *Episcia dianthiflora, Selaginella,* strawberry saxifrage, *Oxalis,* myrtle, or wandering jew. For contrast and variety use taller plants, such as begonias, fittonias, African violets, small ferns, prayer plant, and watermelon peperomia.

Instead of buying plants, you might prefer to follow up some of the projects in Parts One and Two of this book by planting in the terrarium seeds the children have collected or cuttings they have made. A terrarium is the ideal container for propagating seeds and cuttings: it provides the moist, sheltered environment in which they thrive. Obviously seeds like the avocado are too big for terrarium planting, but tree seeds, fruit seeds, or any seed of a small plant will flourish in a cultivated garden terrarium. Once seedlings grow too tall for the terrarium, they can be dug up and potted individually. Instead of transplanting rooted cuttings of small plants to individual pots, you can also grow them in your terrarium. Simply dig holes in the terrarium soil and insert them. Cuttings from wandering jews, begonias, peperomias, ivy, ferns, flame violets, kangaroo vines, African violets, prayer plants, philodendrons, and saxifrages are a good size for terrarium growing.

Equipment:
1. A clean terrarium case prepared with a base of gravel, sand and charcoal for drainage. (Follow the procedures described in the Woodland terrarium project.)
2. Moist potting soil.
3. A collection of plants of various heights, colors, and textures, or a variety of seeds, or rooted cuttings.
4. A clothes sprinkler or syringe.

Method:
1. Over the drainage base put a two to three-inch layer of potting soil. Contour the soil so that it is higher at the back or sides.
2. If you are using potted plants, knock them out of their pots by holding them upside down in one hand with your fingers spread over the top to support the plant, and sharply tapping the bottoms of the pots with a trowel or other instrument held in the other hand. Keep the soil intact around the plant's roots.
3. Make holes in the terrarium soil to receive the plants. Without disturbing the roots, set the plants in the holes and firmly press the soil in around them. Make sure no leaves are touching the glass. If you are using seeds or cuttings, follow the direc-

tions for propagating them given in Parts One and Two of this book.
4. Spray the plants lightly with water.
5. Clean the glass and cover the terrarium.
6. Care for the cultivated garden terrarium in the same way as the woodland terrarium.

5. *A Bog Terrarium*

Bog communities are the most unusual and challenging terraria to make. Since bog plants will thrive only in very acid soil, the first difficulty is to provide some. The easiest way is to equip yourself with a plastic container and get some muck from a swamp or stream bank where there is plenty of dead organic matter: In effect, bring the bog to the terrarium. If this is impossible, you may send away for bog soil or make do with sphagnum moss.

Bog plants are not only particular about their conditions, they are also exotic—and fascinating to children. They consist largely of such insectivorous species as Venus' flytrap, pitcher plant, and sundew. Finding specimens of them in nature or in plant stores may be as difficult as acquiring bog soil. If so, they are available for under ten dollars in a kit that includes both plants and a bag of bog soil; to get this kit write to:

General Biological Supply House
8200 South Hoyne Avenue
Chicago, Illinois 60620
or
Carolina Biological Supply Company
Burlington, North Carolina 27215

Call your local horticultural society for other sources.

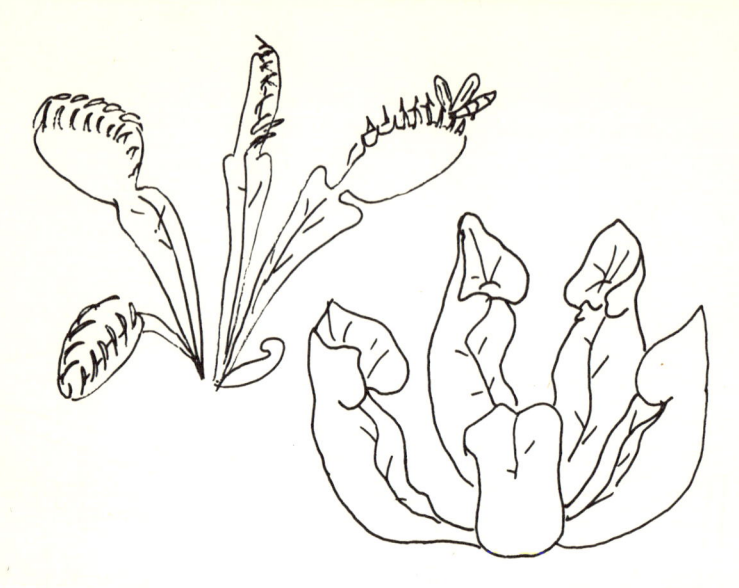

The modified leaves of carnivorous plants: Venus' flytrap on the left and pitcher plant on the right.

Equipment:
1. A clean terrarium case lined with gravel, sand, and charcoal. (Follow the procedures described in the Woodland Terrarium project.)
2. Sphagnum moss.
3. Bog plants—Venus' flytrap, pitcher plant, sundew.
4. (Optional) A moisture-loving small animal: a newt, salamander, or toad.

Method:
1. Cover the drainage material with a two-inch mat of sphagnum, using either living or dried material.
2. Thoroughly soak the sphagnum, allowing some moisture to seep into the drainage material.

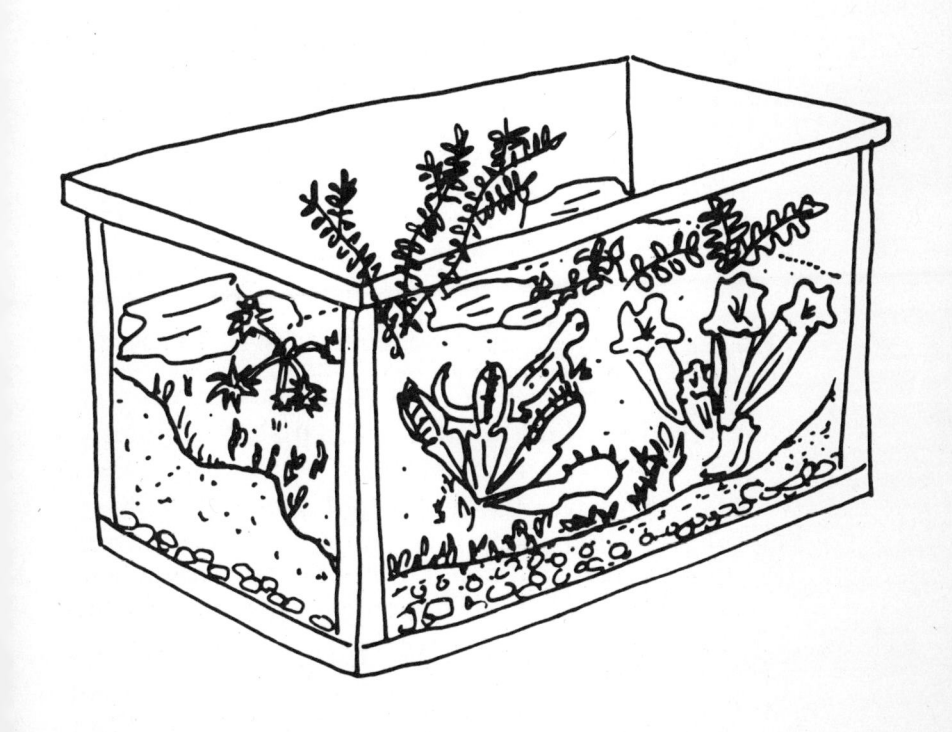

A bog terrarium inhabited by a newt and planted with carnivorous plants, hemlock and blueberry seedlings, ferns, and mosses.

3. Make deep holes for the Venus' flytrap and pitcher plant, which have deep roots. Make shallower holes for the sundew. Set in the plants, cover the roots with sphagnum, and press firmly in place. If you have a large container, you may want to make a natural setting by creating a rocky cliff with hemlock, cypress, swamp azalea, or juniper leading into the bog. Build up the slope using two parts acid soil to one part sphagnum, mixed thoroughly. Plant sundews on the higher ground along with hemlock seedlings, and tiny blueberry or cranberry bushes. Look for these plants in the wild, but don't expect them to bear fruit indoors.
4. Clean the glass, cover the terrarium, and place it in a cool location.

6. Dish Gardens

The miniature garden, or dish garden, is really an open terrarium. Like a terrarium, a dish garden must make sense as an ecosystem: A cactus and a woodland fern would neither look good nor do well together in a dish garden any more than they would in a closed terrarium.

Part of the fun of making a dish garden is searching for the right kind of container. Children should look around their houses to see what they can find: a chipped cereal bowl, a deep saucer, an old platter, a discarded metal tray or a cookie tin will all do as long as they are deep enough to hold soil. It is best to choose an inconspicuous container that does not detract attention from the plant arrangement.

Two kinds of ecosystems do well in dish gardens: cultivated gardens and desert communities. Bog and woodland communities would not succeed in the dry, overheated air of most homes and schools.

A cultivated dish garden growing in a cookie tin. It is planted, from left to right, with a prayer plant, wandering jew, and peperomia.

A Cultivated Dish Garden

Equipment:
1. A clean container.
2. Drainage material—pebbles, gravel, broken pots.
3. Potting soil. If you mix your own soil, use
    1 part sand
    2 parts loam
    1 part leaf mold
    ½ part dried cow manure (optional; available in garden supply stores)
    1 tablespoon bone meal
    a few pieces of charcoal
  If you purchase potting soil in a bag, mix it with equal parts coarse sand and add charcoal.
4. A collection of tiny plants in two-inch pots. Choose plants that offer variety in color and shape. Avoid using only tall, stiff plants or only short, sprawling plants. Make sure that the plants you choose have about the same moisture and light requirements. In a sunny location *Peperomia*, prayer plant, artillery plant, *Cissus*, *Hoya*, wandering jew, grape ivy, coleus and jade plant all go well together. *Pilea*, *Philodendron*, *Begonia*, *Peperomia*, baby's tears, *Fittonia*, and flame violet will do well in low light.

Dish garden plants may also be grown from seeds or cuttings, following the directions in Parts One and Two of this book.

Method:
1. Place a layer of drainage material in the container and add the potting soil up to about one-half inch from the rim.

2. Dig holes for the plants and set them in. For convenience, you may bury them in their pots. The plants will do better if you turn them out of the pots before planting them, but be sure to keep the soil ball around the roots intact.
3. Water the dish garden sparingly as needed. To determine if watering is necessary, test the soil with your finger.
4. Give the plants a few hours of sunlight each day, and keep the foliage clean by occasional syringing.
5. When the plants grow too large for the dish, dig them up and transfer them to larger pots. Replace them with rooted cuttings.

A Desert Dish Garden

Equipment
1. A clean, shallow container provided with drainage.
2. Cactus potting soil. If you mix your own, use

   3 parts garden soil (preferably sterile)

   1 part leaf mold

   ½ part sharp sand (available in aquarium-supply stores)

   ½ part crushed limestone (available in hardware and garden-supply stores)

   ½ part crushed brick (you can crush brick yourself with a hammer)

   A pinch of dried cigarette or pipe tobacco to inhibit root lice
3. A collection of tiny cacti or other succulents (plants with fleshy leaves or stems) in small pots. Avoid cacti with spines. (See Project 2 for a list of suggested plants. You can use seeds or cuttings if you prefer, following the directions in Parts One and Two of this book.)

A desert dish garden planted in an orange crate. Growing in it are, from left to right, Crassula schmidtii, Sedum sieboldii, Hawthoria *(zebra plant)*, Gasteria liliputana, and Lithops *(living stone)*.

Method:
1. Plant the succulents as in the cultivated-garden project.
2. Water the desert garden infrequently but heavily. Really pour as much water as you can into the garden, wait ten minutes, then tip the dish on its side and pour off the excess. Do not water again until the soil is completely dry. Since the desert gets sudden downpours of rain, this method is better for desert plants than the frequent light waterings you would give other plant communities.
3. Use no fertilizer for the first year. The second year add a mild liquid fertilizer monthly.

SOME QUESTIONS AND ANSWERS ABOUT TERRARIA AND PLANT COMMUNITIES

How can animals breathe in a closed terrarium? Why don't they smother?

The ability of animals to live in a closed terrarium illustrates a basic ecological principle. Green plants, using light energy and carbon dioxide, are able to make their own food, a simple sugar called glucose. In this process, which is known as photosynthesis, oxygen is given off. The animal uses the oxygen when it breathes, and gives off carbon dioxide, which is in turn used by the plant in photosynthesis. Plants need oxygen, too, to use the food they make during photosynthesis, but they give off more oxygen than they need, and the excess is available to animals. This interaction is an excellent example of nature's balance. Of course you could not crowd a small terrarium with animals, because there would not be enough oxygen for all of them; you would be creating an ecologically unbalanced community.

Why doesn't a closed terrarium need to be watered?

In a closed terrarium you have an example of a hydrological, or water, cycle. The stages of this cycle are evaporation, condensation, and precipitation.

In a terrarium the water in the soil and the water from the plants evaporate into the air. The vapor condenses on the glass, as it would in clouds, and precipitates, or "rains," back onto the soil, which absorbs it. The roots of the plants take in the water, which is carried through the vascular system (i.e., the veins) to all parts of the plant. The excess is given off as water vapor through tiny openings on the surfaces of the leaves, and the cycle begins again.

If the condensation on the sides of your terrarium is excessive, you can open the cover to allow some of the water vapor escape. This simulates the effect of a sudden breeze on a humid day.

If a terrarium is an ecological community, why does supplementary food need to be added for animals?

In an ecosystem there is a natural food chain: Plants produce energy; many tiny insects and herbivores eat the plants, and they in turn are the food for a few carnivores. In a home terrarium you are limiting the number of herbivores, or insects.

Therefore, there is an insufficient energy or food supply for a toad or carnivore of similar size.

How do you propagate mealworms to feed terrarium animals?

In order to propagate mealworms, buy about two or three dozen where you buy your terrarium animal. The mealworms are actually larvae of beetles. Get a covered gallon tin, fill it half-full of oatmeal or cornmeal or a mixture of the two. Add half a potato, a carrot, or a piece of apple to supply moisture. Make some strips from newspaper, crumple them, and add them, along with the mealworms, to the tin. The larvae will feed, grow, pupate, and emerge as black beetles. They will then lay eggs and the life cycle will begin again.

The beetles crawl but do not fly, so it is a good idea to secure a piece of cheesecloth with a rubber band over the top of the tin. Make sure that air can get in—and that the beetles can't get out! In a month you will have a good supply of mealworms to feed your terrarium animals.

Feel free to remove as many mealworms as you need to feed your terrarium animal, but try not to stir things up too much in their nest. About once a month add a handful of meal and a slice of potato. In six months or so, when the tin smells really bad from the droppings of the insects, turn the contents out onto spread newspapers, refill the container with fresh meal and newspaper, replace the worms, beetles, and eggs, and begin again.

Although this procedure may not appeal to the

squeamish, who can buy mealworms as they need them from a pet store, it is a fascinating way for children to learn about the life cycle of insects.

Why should the leaves of plants in a terrarium not touch the glass?
The glass gets very hot if it is in the sunlight. The foliage would literally cook.

Will the insectivorous bog plants survive if they are not supplied with insects?
Carnivorous plants have poorly developed root systems and grow in soils deficient in nitrogen. The insects they digest and absorb give them a supplementary supply of nitrogen and other minerals they lack. The plants are green, however, and can therefore carry on photosynthesis, grow, and produce flowers and seeds even though they may be deprived of animal food. In other words, the carnivorous habit is useful, but not essential to the plant.

Appendix A
Common Poisonous Plants

Although horticulture is surely the least dangerous of hobbies, it is a good idea for parents and teachers to be aware that a few plants commonly found around the house may be poisonous. Children (and household pets, too) who are plant lovers in the gastronomical sense should be kept away from certain kinds of seeds, fruit, flowers, and foliage.

1. Apple seeds and apricot and peach kernels *(Rosaceae)* all contain cyanide. A man who found apple seeds a delicacy saved a cupful to eat and died of cyanide poisoning.

2. Autumn crocus *(Colchicum autumnale)* should not be in a house with small children or plant-eating pets. Any part of the plant is poisonous if eaten.

3. Dumb cane *(Dieffenbachia)* contains sap toxic in open cuts. Be careful when removing leaves or cutting the cane. Wear gloves if you want to try air layering. *Dieffenbachia* gets its common name, dumb cane, because if it is bitten or chewed, it causes a swelling of the tongue so serious that the victim cannot speak.

4. European beech *(Fagus sylvatica)*, unlike the native American beech *(Fagus gradifolia)*, produces poisonous seeds.

5. Horse chestnut *(Aesculus hippocastanium)* nuts are poisonous. Those delicious chestnuts you roast on winter days are from the true chestnut tree *(Castanea)*.

6. Jerusalem cherry *(Solanum pseudo-capsicum)* is a popular plant at Christmastime because of its bright cherrylike fruit. These berries are tempting, but poisonous if eaten. They may cause a rash when touched; wear gloves around them.

7. Lantana, an attractive flowering house or garden plant, produces berries that are toxic if eaten.

8. Lily-of-the-valley *(Convallaria majalis)* bears red berries, after the flowers die, that are poisonous.

9. Mango stems contain a poison very similar to that of poison ivy, and the skin of the fruit sometimes contains traces. Do not eat the skin, and wear rubber gloves when cleaning the pit to plant it.

10. Mistletoe berries are poisonous when eaten.

11. Oleander *(Nerium oleander)* is a popular flowering plant so lethal that even using the twigs of the plant to roast hot dogs can cause poisoning. Eating one leaf can kill a man. Obviously these plants don't belong around children.

12. Potatoes, though they are staples of our diet, have poisonous greens: vines, sprouts, sun-greened skin, and uncooled peelings are all toxic if eaten.

13. *Philodendron*, one of the hardiest and most common houseplants, contains calcium oxalate. Cats have been known to be poisoned from eating the leaves.

14. Primula, a beautiful and popular spring flowering plant, causes allergic reactions in some people, who develop poison-ivy-like rashes.

Appendix B
Where to Send for Plants and Supplies

I. *Seeds*

W. ATLEE BURPEE CO.
Philadelphia, Pa. 19132
  or
Clinton, Iowa 52732
  or
Riverside, Calif. 92502

EVANS PLANT CO.
Dept. 5
Ty Ty, Ga. 31795
  (vegetables only)

HORTICULTURAL
  ENTERPRISES
Dept. H
P.O. Box 34082
Dallas, Texas

LAVONNE'S GREENHOUSE
463 2nd Ave.
Riddle, Ore. 97469

OROL LEDEN & SONS
Center St.
Sewell, N.J. 08080

GEO. W. PARK SEED CO.
P.O. Box 31
Greenwood, S.C. 29646

SEEDWAY, INC.
1184
Hall, N.Y. 14463

II. *Bulbs*

ANTONELLI BROS.
2545 Capitola Rd.
Santa Cruz, Calif. 95060

INTER-STATE NURSERIES, INC.
Hamburg, Iowa 51640

P. DE JAGER & SONS
Dept. H-2734
South Hamilton, Mass. 01982

III. *Carnivorous Plants*

CAROLINA BIOLOGICAL
  SUPPLY HOUSE
Burlington, N.C. 27215

GENERAL BIOLOGICAL
  SUPPLY HOUSE
8200 South Hoyne Ave.
Chicago, Ill. 60620

PETER PAULS NURSERIES
Darcy Rd.
Canandaigua, N.Y. 14424

IV. *Terrarium Supplies*

ALLGROVE
Box 459 H
Wilmington, Mass. 01887
  (catalog 25 cents)

ARMSTRONG ASSOCIATES, INC.
Box 127
Basking Ridge, N.J. 07920

MARKO
94 Porete Ave.
North Arlington, N.J. 07032

V. *General Supplies*

CASCHETTO
396 H Clark St.
Bridgeport, Conn. 06606

HOUSE PLANT CORNER
Oxford, Md. 21654

INDEX

Acacia, 77
Acorn, 26
African violets, 110, 153
Ailanthus, 76
Alder, 77
Algae, 28
Aluminum foil, 19
Anatomy of a Seed (project), 33–35
Animals, in terrariums, 145–46, 149–50, 163–66
Apple, 26, 77, 81, 87; McIntosh, 88
Apricot, 58
April in February (project), 102–5
Artillery plant, 160
Ash, 76–77
Aspen, 83
Aspidistra. See Cast-iron plant
Auxins, 56
Avocado, 48, 51, 58, 87, 153
Avocados (project), 47–51
Azalea, 84; swamp, 150

Baby tears, 160
Banana, 58, 87–88
Barley, 58
Basswood, 77
Beans, 26, 29, 32, 33–35, 37, 45
Beech, 76–77

Beetles, black. See Mealworms
Beets, 64, 112, 114–17
Begonia Garden (project), 130–32
Begonias, 90, 110, 128–32, 153, 160
Biennials, 112
Birdseed, 40
Bits that Grow Big (project), 126–28
Blueberries, 26
Blueberry bushes, 158
Bog Terrarium (project), 155–58
Bottle caps, 19
Bulbs, 100, 106; forcing of, 102–4
Burro-tails, 145

Cabbage, dwarf, 63
Cactus, 145, 158
California redbud tree, 77
Callus formation, 132
Camellias, 105
Cantaloupe, midget, 63
Cardinal's cap, 145
Carnivorous plants, 166. See also Bog Terrarium
Carraway seeds, 58
Carrot and Beet Garden (project), 115–16
Carrot Hanging Basket (Project), 116–18

172 COMPLETE BOOK OF FLOWERPOT ECOLOGY

Carrots, 63–64, 112, 115–18
Cast-iron plant, 96
Catalpa, 76
Chameleon, 149–50
Charcoal, 55
Cherry, 26, 58, 77; minitree, 81; wild, 76
Chick-peas, 58
Chives, 63–64
Cissus, 160
Citrus fruit, 43, 87
Citrus Groves (project), 43–45
Clone, 88
Coconut, 29
Coffee beans, 58
Coleus, 90, 105, 107, 133, 160
Containers, types of, 15–20
Corn kernels, 19, 32, 33–35
Corn, midget, 63
Cotoneaster, 84
Cotyledons, 34–35, 56
Cranberry bushes, 158
Cress, 36, 40
Cucumbers, 26, 42, 45, 47, 58, 64; Cherokee, 63
Cultivated Dish Garden (project), 158–61
Cultivated Garden Terrarium. See Garden Terrarium (project)
Cuttings, 89–93, 96–97, 105–7, 119, 153–54. See also Leaf Cuttings in Soil or Water (project); Leaves, cutting
Cypress, 158

Daffodils, 102
Dates, 58, 87
Deciduous trees, 82
Desert Dish Garden (project), 161–63
Desert Terrarium (project), 145–46
Dill, 58

Dioecious trees, 76
Dish gardens, 157–63. See also Terrariums
Drainage, 18
Dwarfing, 84. See also Pruning

Ecology, 148
Ecosystem, 137, 158
Egg Carton Gardens (project), 37–39
Eggplant, midget, 63
Eggshells, 20, 37–39
Elm, 83
Episcias, 153
Evergreens, 76, 77, 83; Chinese, 96, 133, 153

Ferns, 28, 110, 146, 149, 153, 158; Boston, 153
Fertilization, 26
Fertilizers, 20, 69, 72–73
Figs, 87; pasteurized, 58
Fir, 77
Fittonias, 153, 160
Flame violets, 160
Flats, covering of, 56; planting of, 64–68
Flower, definition of, 26; low growing, 42
Flowering cycle, 25–26
Forcing, 102–5, 106
Fruit, 26, 27. See also specific fruits
Fungi, 28
Fuchsia, 90

Garden Terrarium (project), 153–55
Gardening tools, household, 18–20
Gardens, miniature. See Dish gardens; Minifarms; Terrariums
Geraniums, 90

Geotropsim, 117
Germination, 32, 48, 51–52, 58–59, 64, 72, 77–78, 78, 107, 119
Ginger root, 96
Gingkoes, 76
Glass jars, use of, 19
Grapefruit, 43
Grape ivy, 160
Grapes, 45
Grass, 36, 40
Groats, 58

Hackberries, 76
Hemlock, 77, 149, 158
Hen-and-chickens, 96
Herbs, 42, 64
Hickory, 76
Holly, 105
Hormones, 55, 90, 105; rooting, 106–7, 121
Horse chestnut, 75, 77
Horsetails, 28
Houseleek. *See* Hen-and-chickens
Hoya, 160
Hyacinths, 87, 102
Hybridization, 58, 107
Hydrological cycle, 164

Impatiens, 42, 90
Insecticides, 71
Insects, 20, 69, 71, 145, 150, 166

Jade plant, 160
Japanese garden, 81
Jasmine, 84
Jelly-bean plant, 145
Juniper, 84, 149, 158

Kale, 63–64
Kalenchoe, 145
Kentucky coffee tree, 76–77

Kumquat, 43

Labeling, 64
Ladybug, 71
Landscaping, 80–81, 150
Laurel, 149
Leaf Cuttings in Soil or Water (project), 122–26
Leaf mold, 149
Leaves, cuttings, 121–33. *See also* True leaf
Lemon, 43
Lentils, 32, 37, 58
Lettuce, 36, 40; for minifarm, 63–64
Lichens, 28, 149
Lilies of the valley, 96
Lime, 43, 88
Liverworts, 149
Lobelia, 42
Locust, 76–77

Magnolia, 77
Mangrove, 77
Maple, 75–77, 149
Marigolds, 37
Marijuana, 40
McIntosh, John, 88
Mealworms, 145, 150; propagation, 165–66
Meristematic tissue, 105–6, 133
Mesquite, 77
Minifarm, 61–73
  care of, 69–73
  planting of, 65–69, 72
  seeds for, 63–64
Miniforest, 75–84
  care of, 82
  dwarfing, 79, 82, 84
  landscaping, 80–81
  planting, 77–78, 81, 83–84
  seed hunting, 75–76

trees and shrubs for, 75–77, 81, 84
Miniorchard, 81
Mint, 42
Molds, 28, 53–55
Mosses, 28, 146, 149
Mustard plant, 36, 40, 64
Myrtle, 153

Narcissus bulbs, 102–5
Nasturtiums, 37, 42, 90
Newt, 149, 156
Nitrogen, 72, 166
Nodes, 96, 105–6
Nuts, 58

Oak, 75–76, 83, 149
Oats, 58
Onion Bouquet (project), 100–2
Onions, 107–8
Orange, 43, 51
Oxalis, 153

Palm, 77
Parakeet seeds, 40
Parent plant, 88, 95–96
Parsley, 42, 63–64
Parsnips, 112, 115, 117
Pear, 26, 77, 87; tree, 81
Peas, 37, 45, 51; midget, 63
Peat moss, 20, 65–66
Peperomia, 160
Peppers, 64
Perlite, 20
Persimmon, 58
Philodendron, 96, 133, 160
Phosphorus, 72–73
Photosynthesis, 112, 163
Pilea, 160
Pinching off. *See* Pruning
Pineapple, 87–88
Pine

forest, 81
needles, 149
White, 77
Pitcher plant, 155–58
Plaintain, 58
Plant collecting, 148–49
Plant containers. *See* Containers, types of
Plant propagation, 25, 28, 61, 109
Plastic bags, 18–19
Plastic-Bottle Strawberry Jar (project), 40–42
Plum, 26, 58, 77; minitree, 81
Poisonous plants, list of, 167–68
Pomegranate, 58
Popcorn, 32
Poplar, 76–77
Poppy seed, 58
Popsicle sticks, 18, 40
Potassium, 72–73
Potato Heads (project), 36–37
Potato Patch (project), 99–100
Potatoes, 87, 106, 107, 112
Pothos, 96, 133
Potting soil. *See* Soil, potting
Prayer plant, 153, 160
Propagation of plants. *See* Plant propagation
Pruning, 56, 79, 82, 84

Quince, 84

Radishes, 63–64, 112, 115
Rhizome Rearing (project), 96–97
Rice, 58
Root Division (project), 110–11
Rooting medium, 133
Roots, 109–19
    and gravity, 52–53, 117
    fibrous, 109, 119
    storage, 109, 112, 115, 117, 119
Runners. *See* Stolon rooting

Rye seed, 40

Salamander, 150, 156
Sansevieria, 96, 110, 132
Sassafras, 76–77
Savory seed, 42
Seaweed, 28
Seed Hunt (project), 29, 58. See also Miniforest, seed hunting
Seeds, 25–59. See also Germination; Minifarm; Miniforest
  and gravity, 52–53, 117
  and molds, 53–54
  description, 25, 26, 29, 34–35, 58–59
  covering of, 56
  freezing, 78
  growth, 51–52, 56
  planting, 54–59
  quick-growing, 36, 40, 43, 45
  in terrariums, 153
Selaginella, 149, 153
Sempervivum. See Hen-and-chickens
Shrubs, 84
Snake, 149–50
Snake plant. See Sansevieria
Soil, potting
  acidic (bog soil), 155
  cactus mix, 145, 161
  home mixing of, 160, 161
  home sterilization, 54–55
  recommended, 20, 62
Soy bean seed, 58
Sphagnum moss, 155, 156, 158
Sponge Garden (project), 39–40
Spray bottles, 20
Spruce, 149
Squash, 45, 47, 64
Stems
  and gravity, 53
  underground, 96, 99, 100, 112

Stolon Rooting (project), 95–96
Strawberries, 58
Strawberry Jar project. See Plastic-Bottle Strawberry Jar
Strawberry saxifrage, 153
Succulent plants, 145, 161–63
Sundew, 155–56, 158
Sunflower seed, 58
Sweet alyssum, 42
Sweetgum seed, 77
Sweet Potato Vine (project), 112–14, 119
Swiss chard, 64
Sycamore, 77

Tangerine, 43
Terminal bud, 56, 79, 82
Terrarium case, building of, 139–44
Terrariums, 137–57, 163–66. See also Animals, in terrariums; Dish gardens
  bog, 155–58
  cuttings for, 154
  desert, 145–46, 158
  drainage, 145–46
  foliage, 166
  garden, 153–55
  open, 158
  seeds for, 153
  water and air in, 163–64
  woodland, 146–51, 158
Thyme seed, 42
Toad, 145, 149–50, 156
Tomato, 42, 58, 63, 64
Tools, gardening. See Gardening tools
Trading Slips Club (project), 89–93
Transplanting
  of minitrees, 81, 83–84

of seedlings, 39, 45, 69, 78
  to terrariums, 154
Tree frog, 149–50
Trees. *See* Miniforest
Trees of North America (Brockman), 83
Triangles (leaf cuttings project), 128–30
True leaf, 56, 83
Tuber, 99, 107
Tulips, 102
Tumbler Gardens (project), 32–33
Turnips, 112, 115–17

Vegetables, 28, 61–73
Vegetative propagation, 28, 87–88; projects, 89–107
Venus flytrap, 155–56 158
Vermiculite, 20
Vinca, 42

Vine Salad "Trees" (project), 45–47
Walnut, 26, 76, 83
Wandering Jew, 90, 105, 133, 153, 160
Water cycle. *See* Hydrological cycle
Watering, 69–71
Watermelon, 45, 47, 58; yellow, 63
Watermelon peperomia, 153
Willow, 76
Woodland Terrarium (project), 146–51

Yeast, 28
Yew, 84, 105

Zinnias, 37